Girl, Get Your Mind Right!

HARPER

NEW YORK . LONDON . TORONTO . SYDNEY

THE TELL-IT-LIKE-IT-IS ADVICE
YOUR LOVE LIFE HAS BEEN MISSING

Girl, Get Your Mind Right!

Tionna Tee Smalls

HARPER

This book is written as a source of information only. The information in this book has been carefully researched, and all efforts have been made to ensure accuracy. The authors and the publisher assume no responsibility for any injuries suffered or damages or losses incurred during or as a result of following this information. All information should be carefully studied and clearly understood before taking any action based on the information or advice in this book.

GIRL, GET YOUR MIND RIGHT! Copyright © 2011 by Tionna Tee Smalls. All rights reserved. Printed in the United States of America. No part of this book may be used or reproduced in any manner whatsoever without written permission except in the case of brief quotations embodied in critical articles and reviews. For information address HarperCollins Publishers, 10 East 53rd Street, New York, NY 10022.

HarperCollins books may be purchased for educational, business, or sales promotional use. For information please write: Special Markets Department, HarperCollins Publishers, 10 East 53rd Street, New York, NY 10022.

FIRST EDITION

Designed by Janet M. Evans

Library of Congress Cataloging-in-Publication Data is available upon request.

ISBN 978-0-06-203284-3

11 12 13 14 15   OV/RRD   10 9 8 7 6 5 4 3 2 1

*For every woman who
has had enough*

CONTENTS

CONTENTS

✦ PREFACE
What I Have Learned

THIS IS THE OPINION OF TIONNA TEE SMALLS. YOU CAN choose to not listen to any of the advice you read in this book, but your love life will remain the same; trust me. If you're one of the millions of women in the world who are tired of the games, the lies, the bullcrap, then take your hand and wrap it around this book. *Girl, Get Your Mind Right!* is now your dating and relationship bible. Now girl, get your mind right and be the lady you want to be: a warrior, bitch, a princess, or a superstar. It's time to get your mind right. You are what you say you are, and girlfriend, you can do everything that you say you can do. It is time to stop blaming him for your problems and it is time to figure out why you sleep alone in a bed big enough for two. The Girl, Get Your Mind Right! campaign has begun.

When I wrote the first version of this book I had been hurt really badly by loser men and I had a lot of anger. I was determined to save all the women in the world from the mistakes that I had made. I had the vision of helping women not fall for the okie-doke of a loser man. I thought all I had to do was tell my story and women would immediately step up their game and heed the advice. Now three years later, my life is much brighter and I can see that there are many good men out there. We just don't always see them. I also can't wave my wand and make all women take responsibility for their relationships. It isn't that simple. But with this new book and my new outlook, I am ready to do what I can—and right here right now, we are going to start the Girl, Get Your Mind Right! movement.

✦ INTRODUCTION
Girl, It Is Time To Get Your Mind Right!

IT IS TIME FOR YOU TO STOP FEELING SORRY FOR YOUR love life and look into why you are attracting the wrong guys in the first place. We don't realize that most of the times we are in bad relationships because we want to be in bad relationships.

I learned a long time ago that life is all about choices and we live and die by the choices we make. If you choose to stay and stick it out with a loser, then that's on you. If you choose to try to change someone that you already know is not right for you, then that's on you, because it doesn't take a genius to know that people don't change unless they want to. Most of the women I meet are pretty good women who dream of finding the right man. They are beautiful, motivated, employed, and most of all, they want love. But they are looking for it in all the wrong places and many of them don't know what they want from a relationship. Some women say that they want a nice guy, yet they are the same ones who like when a man pulls their weave, smacks 'em up, and disrespects them. That right there is a contradiction in itself and a confliction of thoughts. He can't be nice if he's going to whip your ass (point-blank period). It's time for us women to know exactly what it is we want from the men in our life. If we want a good man, it's time for us to get "good" ourselves. We have to understand that we are what we attract. If you are constantly attracting the wrong man; chances are you are giving off something that is allowing for these people to come into your life.

You also need to get rid of the "super-save-a-ho" attitude. Yes, I know you want to help a man and bring him up to your level, upgrade him but can't. You meet a guy with no job and then try to hook up his resumé and send it out to employers for him. He doesn't have to do anything but wear a button-up shirt and go to the interview. Or you offer a man who suffers from "walk-itis" (my word for a man who doesn't own a car) a car. You try to make yourself feel better by saying, "Oh, I just got him a hooptie." Yes, it's a hooptie, but a hooptie is still a car; a car he didn't have until he met your nice ass. You got him the car thinking that he would be able to take care of his business better if he had a ride, but he doesn't do that. Like the guys who drive their girl's car all day while she's at work, he uses that old automobile to take other chicks to work and to go and get his freak on at another broad's house.

The sad thing is the game never changes, just the situations, and you, my friend, have been in the same situation time after time with guys who weren't even worthy of smelling the coochie, much less being the main thing you live your life for. You gave a loser man mobility and there is nothing worse than that. He dupes you and you continue to ask yourself, "Why me?" not ever asking, "Why not me?" Sister, what are you doing to avoid getting into the same *ish* every time you meet a potential new boo? Ask yourself, are you giving up the booty too quick? Are you letting him know what makes you tick too soon? Or are you just falling for every guy you give your drawers up to? For most of us, one of these problems is the reason why we don't have a good man, and some suffer from all three of these love fallacies.

I am tired of women accepting bullcrap from these two-bit effing men. I understand it's a man shortage and all, but it's really time to put your Gucci-shoe-wearing foot down and say, "No more." It's definitely more easily said than done, but right here, right now, we are all taking an oath of strength because we are all the shit and we all deserve better. Yes . . . fat, skinny, bald headed, it doesn't matter. You can step your game up and get yourself together and bag the man you want to have. Get him right, train him, and keep him as your man. Sit down and allow yourself to be tasted and enjoyed. Aren't you tired of being duped and taken advantage of? I know you are, because your friends are tired for you. It is really time for you to be the chick you always wanted to be, because you, my friend, deserve it and the new you is reachable if you just take the time out and get *you* together.

You can't get the guy you want, be a good woman to a man, or be in a relationship with anyone if you are not the person you really want to be in life. You can't live up to other people's standards or views about yourself.

If you know you haven't quite loved yourself the best in a while, sit down and relax, because you are just a mere work in progress, and things will work out for you in just a jiffy as long as you be real with yourself and accept the things you do negatively within yourself. Now if he doesn't love and appreciate that, then it's definitely his loss. When does a woman say, "No more"? Ladies, no matter how many men have done you wrong, your time is not up. I don't care how old you think you are, there's somebody out there for you, but you have to be ready for it. Yes, I said it, you have to be ready, because some of us wouldn't recognize a good man if he came and smacked us on the head with his penis.

The right man may be right under your nose, but are you mature enough to receive him or are you still running the hills looking for a man who you think may be able to one day be Mr. Right? Well, I am going to help you find Mr. Right and help you keep him. All men like coochie, and you, my friend, are the person who has it, but don't think you can snag that guy just because you have that coochie. You can only snag him if he cares about you and wants to be with you, and that, my friend, takes getting into that man's mental, and getting into a man's brain is one tough task, but you can do it if your game is tight.

It is time to get your mind right and you won't be happy until you make yourself happy. We often look at men to make us happy, but every woman who does this ends up unhappy. A man can never make you happy; besides, making you happy eternally isn't his job (believe it or not). It's your job, as you need to find joy outside of him and if he's the only source of your happiness, what are you going to do if he's gone? So let's get our minds right, each one of us, to heal ourselves, make us better women, and help all the little girls who look up to us.

I wrote this book not only because I wanted you to be able to get over all of the things that are hindering you from love but because I wanted you to be able to be strong enough and confident enough to enjoy love in your life. Sad, but most women who go through stuff with no-good men are so afraid to share their love.

As I always tell women who are hanging on to heartbreaks they had over the years: if you never allow love into your life after him, he's winning. Yes, most people who have broken your heart in the past get off on your misery. If you become happy their impact isn't valid. Once you are happy, you forget everything bad that has ever happened in your life. So I want you to become happy. I want you to revive the faith you once had in love because true love still—and will always—exists. You just have to have an open heart.

Time for a little tough love . . .

Stop Messing Up
Your Mind

Rule
#1

A "mind wrecker" is a man who will do anything to mess up your soul and make you feel mentally small. He is a manipulator, a liar, a lame, and overall a game player. You have been dealing with this man and still you don't know your place in his heart. He compliments you sometimes to cover up his real jealousy and ill will he has against you. He will take any chance that he has to make you feel down, because he knows how to make you tick. This Mind Wrecker will make you feel like you're his queen in front of other people, but when you two are alone, he does little things that make you wonder what his true intentions are. This is a man who wants to isolate you and keep you all to himself without any of your family or close friends around that can catch him and call him out on his bullshit.

THE MIND WRECKER WANTS TO BREAK YOU AND CONTROL YOU

This Mind Wrecker may not physically put his hands on you, but he will verbally bash you in every argument that you have by calling you a slut, a whore, a side bitch, an ugly bitch, a fat bitch. This Mind Wrecker knows that you're a good catch and secretly admires your drive, your motivation, your confidence, but all the while he hates you for those very same qualities. This man's main goal is to break your brain so that he can take over and conquer you. He will constantly break up with you and only wants to get back when he feels that you're on top and you could live your life without him.

This man loves the way you look but will still go and screw an ugly girl on the side just for kicks because it makes him feel more powerful and less pathetic. This man loves to see you cry and loves to hear you talk smack about your friends and family. He will urge you on even more to get rid of your friends so that he can have the upper hand and therefore be the only source to your heart, happiness, and laughter. He will want you to come home after work, but will be the first person to break his dinner date with you just to go chilling with his boys. He never lets you know his plans ahead of time because he doesn't want you to know his every move, yet he requires that you call him every time you step foot out of the house.

This Mind Wrecker seems confident on the outside with his expensive gear and nice hair, but inside he really doesn't feel worthy of you and knows that he's not on your level, so he will try to knock you down a notch. All he does is bring havoc to your once peaceful life because he likes to see you fight emotionally and physically for his love; and you work with him anyway, hoping it won't be like this is forever, but the very sad thing is that he is never going to change.

He will screw your emotions up so much that you will not be the nice quiet girl you once were; you will be a mad bitch to everyone around you, while you will still bow down and take his bullcrap. Before you dated him, you saw life as one big, beautiful, adventurous place; if you didn't get something you wanted, you said, "Oh well, let me try again," but after messing with this negative ass man, you're miserable and the glass is no longer half full to you, it's half empty and you see everything as one big black hole.

This Mind Wrecker makes you so paranoid that every time he's away from you, you believe he is doing something sexual with another, yet you're too afraid to ask him about it. He loves when he gets you crazy so he will play on it even more by not answering his phone and pretending to be asleep when you call only to piss your whole night and early morning off. Therefore, you go to work upset and worried about what's he doing and not focused on what you're supposed to be focused on—your money. He is a Mind Wrecker, so he likes taking over the only place that you can't control, because believe it or not, you can't control what you think about. Then what comes next is a phone call or stupid text saying, *You know I love you, why would I hurt you?* Then you two make plans to meet and talk after work only for him to be back in your bed penetrating your catbag. He's groaning and telling you sweet nothings in your ear, all the while trying to get a nut and think of another master-of-disaster plan on how to get your fine ass off of that pedestal.

The Mind Wrecker uses sex as power. He knows that when you're crying while making love and promising him that you're not going to go anywhere, he's fucking not only your body, but your mind as well. He knows that he's still in charge even though you are on top riding his dick like it's the last thing smoking. And why is he in control? Because we are women and we wear our heart on our sleeves, and many times we mistake sex for love and get gassed up by those four-letter words especially during intimacy. Why else is he in charge? Because he understands that in any love relationship, there is the Lover (the person who gives the love), which is you, and there is the Beloved (the person who receives the love), which is him. He knows that you would do anything for him and that no matter how much he messes up you're always going to take him back after he begs for your forgiveness, and he will be a good boy for a week or two.

This manipulator doesn't love you; hell, he barely takes you seriously. He just wants to get in where he fits in just like everybody else, and it's no longer about sex. He may smile like he believes in you and may taste the inside of your walls but he's waiting for your downfall so that once you're down he can step all over you and make you feel like you never had any existence in his world in the first place. He looks at you as the person who once tried to oppress him and make him feel unworthy with your achievements.

Welcome to the sick world of the man who sleeps with you every night, been with you for years, but still can't stand your freaking guts. It's him, the Mind Wrecker. You love him, you're cosigning his bullshit, but most of all you're fucking him! So ladies, without further interruptions, it's time to stop crying and start doing, because only you can prevent yourself from being a victim of love.

Only you can make the changes you need to make in your life to have a great relationship.

*I*t feels so good when you meet a new guy. Your stomach has butterflies. It's something new and exciting. You have so many plans and expectations for this new fella. You guys exchange numbers, call each other, go on the first date, and your instinct is to light the fuse on the relationship, but you don't yet know how he feels about you and he doesn't know how he feels about you. So slow down. Don't plan out the house, car, and kids quite yet. See how it goes first. See if you actually like him and if he likes you.

Most single women don't take enough time when they first meet a man. They don't take the time to get to know if this is the right someone before they go all head over heels for him. We women believe that everything in the matters of the heart should be rushed because we are afraid that the feeling that we have for a man is going to go somewhere, but we are sadly mistaken.

MALE SHORTAGE OR NOT, YOU HAVE TO TAKE YOUR TIME

I don't know if the male shortage is to blame for why we plan out our whole love life with a man we just met, but we all seem ready to take the big plunge way too soon. I am definitely guilty of doing it too; I had once met a guy and within three weeks had decided he was the one that I wanted and just had to have. I had made plans to be his wife. I just thought oh my God, this is it! I am ready to throw in the towel (Lord, take me now), but I was sadly mistaken. This dude was a loser and if I had taken the time to get to know him and his style, I would have known that he wasn't the man for me in any circumstance. That right there is what I call wasting my brain cells, because all I could do was sit and think about him and how we were going to get this love affair on and popping.

Many of us do it whether we realize we're doing it or not. Don't believe me? Well, think about this: how many times have you gone on one date with a man and the next thing you know, driving home you say, "My mother is going to like him." Wow, you guys just had one date and you are already planning out what you and him are going to wear for Thanksgiving dinner at your parents' house.

It's great you two had fun on one date, but girl, one date is not enough time to determine whether or not he made the cut. These illusions of you guys' future is going to cause you pain and disappointment later when he doesn't live up to the hype. You have to be able to separate your dreams from what is reality. The reality is, he may not want you. He may have had a great first date, but he just sees you as a good friend and maybe a good lay, but he in no way sees you as the chick he wants to walk with down the aisle.

As a woman, I decided to stop dreaming about the fluff (a.k.a. the stuff that I wish would happen) and started thinking about the real (what's in front of me). I advise you to the same. Take your time to figure out how you really feel about him, because believe me, girlfriend, that is exactly what he is doing. Sure, he may be trying to get in your drawers that first night, but he isn't sure exactly how he feels about you as a woman. Those feelings will come clear to him as time goes on. It's time for us women to be smart when making decisions about our heart.

The slower you take things the better for you down the line. Things just end up working out better when you really get to know one another and each other's intentions. You can't know a man's intentions unless you take the time to listen and sees how he treats you.

RELATIONSHIPS FAIL WHEN YOU DON'T KNOW YOUR MAN

You wanted to be with him and he happily obliged; now what? Well, many times, relationships fail because you two didn't really get to know who the other person was before you made the step to being committed. You need to know who the person is before you just give him the pleasure of having the title as your man, because people these days are *7:30* (meaning *crazy*). Most of the times you think you are meeting a nice man but really you are meeting his representative. His getting-in-your-pants, all-nice-and-shit, friendly-persona representative.

When you first met him, he was everything you wanted (so you thought) and that's why you threw in the towel and made him your man, but you later found out he was nothing but a monster. A mean monster who preys on lonely females who snatch him up right away, because they are too desperate to wait for the results of the background check. Ladies, you need to spend time with the man to see how he handles different situations. Remember, zebras can't hide their stripes too long, so eventually the real him will come out. You just watch and see!

TWO YEAR RULE

I used think it took about a year to really get to know someone, but now—I now believe that it takes a lifetime as I have been with my man for over two years now and I think I am just starting to know him. I find out something new about him on a daily basis and he says the same thing about me. The time to get to know someone varies by person so don't think two years is a hard and fast rule. That is just my story. I do believe you will know within six months to a year if this is someone you want to pursue a serious relationship with. This may sound like a long time to you, but there is no bigger decision than deciding on who gets to share your bed. Getting to know someone is more than knowing his favorite color or favorite cereal. It is much deeper than that, it is a mind thing. You have to figure out how these men think, period. You have to really get to know how he handles himself in the world and with others.

SLOW DOWN THE RIDE

When things are getting hot and heavy between you and a new guy, never be afraid to slow down the ride and say, "Hey, I want to get to know you." A real man will respect your wishes and be open to getting to know you and you him. You have to be very wary of any man who rushes into things both physically and emotionally. Sometimes when a man rushes in and calls you his woman or says he loves you, he is just trying to manipulate you for what's in your panties or what's in your pocketbook. We all have come across a man who said he loved us in a matter of weeks or even days and the first thing we think is: he doesn't even know me. Yes, he doesn't know you, so make sure you take a stand against those men who are quick to express emotions because you don't want to be hurt later down the line.

BE CAREFUL OF WHO YOU GIVE YOUR COOKIES TO

Stop making love to every man you go on a date with. You know as women we are very emotional and oftentimes we mistake the feelings we have in the bedroom with the feelings that we have in our heart. You are grown so I am not saying don't give up the cookies, I am saying be careful of who you give your cookies to. Make sure you at least like this person before you jump into bed. Most of the men who I jumped in bed with without thinking were losers or just not the man for me. Some of the men who I allowed in, I knew that they weren't really for me so they don't count, but the one I had the illusion for ended up bad. If I had taken the second to talk more and not quench my horny thirst, I would have known that the guys I dated in the past were not for me.

IF HE LIKES YOU, HE WILL GIVE YOU TIME TO GET TO KNOW HIM

He will let you take your time if he likes you or has any kind of feelings for you. Never rush into things because you are fearful he is going to leave you or go to another woman. He is not the guy for you if he picks up and leaves you for another woman that quick. It is time to stop getting so physical and start talking more. Talking and listening will lead the way for you in your love life. Stop thinking about your wedding on the first date. There is no stopwatch in life when it comes down to matters of the heart.

THE TRUTH WILL COME OUT IN TIME

You have to play the game smart. A man's true self and intentions for you will come out if you just wait a bit to see what he is like. Too many times women make the mistake of loving a man before she even gets a chance to know who he is. Usually when we meet a man, we meet their representative; the person that he wants us to believe he is. You never want to be the person who is hurt just because you didn't take the time out to get to know someone. He can only hide who he is for so long, so be patient, my friend, and wait to see his true self.

WATCH HIM AND HIS CREW!

As important as it is to know him, you've got to also get to know everyone around him, which includes his boys, his mother, and the rest of his family. Who they hang out with usually tells the story of who they are. Sometimes you will meet someone who is reluctant to introduce you to that part of his world and I say watch him. He may be trying to hide something from you if he doesn't want you around the people he holds near and dear to his heart.

GIRL, LISTEN TO HIM!

Most of the times, we meet a man and we are so caught up in how much we like him that we don't listen to anything that is coming out of his mouth. Many times a man says what kind of person he is from the gate—we just don't listen. He may say, "You know, I am not ready to have a girl," or, "I don't want a girl," and we take that as him just talking junk, but lots of times, they are telling the truth. Some men may go on even further, with, "I'm a dog!" If a man says he's a dog or that he is no good, listen to him. Don't ignore what the heck he is saying. Listening to someone is the key if you plan on getting to know him. Stop being so confident with your psychic ability that you think you can tell who he is just by looking at him, because if you don't, you will end up being a sad cookie at the end of the day.

ONCE YOU GET TO KNOW HIM, MAKE THE DECISION IF HE'S THE ONE FOR YOU OR NOT

Now once you get to know him and who he is, you have to make the decision as to whether or not you want to deal with this guy. Sometimes us women convince ourselves of things that we know are straight-up effery. For an example, we date a guy we know does not have the same convictions as us, yet we deal with him because we believe that we can change him or that he will change eventually. Well, it's time for you to decide whether you can deal with a "dog" for the rest of your life—or are you wasting your time with a guy who doesn't have your best interest in mind? The choice you make will be up to you, and hopefully, you will make the right choice—but be clear, you can't make that choice until you really know what his deal is, and you won't find that out until you take your time and dissect the situation. So please, please, please, take your time; it will benefit you in the end.

What you do in the beginning will definitely be your downfall in the end; make the right decisions in the mating and dating stages so you won't suffer later on.

Learn How To Use
the Word No!

Rule
#3

*T*he inability to say no is partly the reason why some women give up the booty to losers and psychos. Saying yes, when our body, mind, and souls are telling us to stay the hell away from this lame is a big problem for us women. It's good to be positive and say yes sometimes, but every guy who comes your way with a smile and some pickup line is not worthy of getting into your short shorts. It's hard to say no, not only because you're horny, but also because you are afraid. Yes, I said it, you're afraid that he won't be interested in talking to you or going on a date with you if you are not having sex with him, but oh well; there are other women out there that he could do it with, so don't let your fear of being rejected stop you from saying no. Sex isn't good when you're under pressure and especially when you don't want to do it. It's best when you feel freaky and free and want to give up the panties. When you're under stress to do it, you can't pretend to enjoy it, never mind orgasm.

A REAL DUDE WILL UNDERSTAND
YOU ARE NOT READY TO HAVE SEX

A good man understands when a lady isn't ready to be intimate and respects it. If your prospective boo ain't hearing that, then move on, girl. There are other fishes out in the sea, ones without all them darn bones. Forcing yourself will only lead you down a road of resentment: resentment toward him and to yourself. I really hate to say this because it's the new millennium and women have the right to be sexually free and all, but ladies, we got to stop giving up the panties so quickly, especially to the guys we like. I was taught that if you like him and want to keep him—you don't give it up; I repeat, you don't give it up. You can get it popping with a jumpoff (a person who is used just for sex) because you don't really like him. But if you really like the guy and want a future with him, you better keep your skirt down and your drawers up.

WAIT UNTIL YOU ARE COMFORTABLE

You have to learn how to say no to temptation and to your horny, lonely thoughts no matter how much you think the feeling is right. A man you adore should never know the material of your underwear before he gets to know you and your most intimate (nonsexual) thoughts. I know this may sound cliché, but giving up the poom poom too quickly may really turn the guy you like off. It's like men lose interest in you when they don't have to work hard to get in you. I'm not saying wait a set amount of months before having sex, because there really is no true science to when you know you are ready or to determine if it will work out, but I am saying wait until you feel comfortable and ready to take that next step. Remember it's your body, so only you can determine when and where to give it up, but homegirl, you better think long and hard before you do it, because having sex is truly an act of spirit transformation. This may sound fruity, but spirit transformation is the act of becoming one with the person you are having sex with and since the guy inserts his penis into your vagina, you literarily receive his spirit—yes even with a condom on. That's why girls who sleep with a lot of men act all confused emotionally and whatnot, because they have too many conflicting souls up in them. That's why I stopped giving it up like that myself (that and a trip to the gynecological office showed me that a vagina is too much of a sensitive place to have just about anyone in it). It's just too much.

If you don't want to have sex with your man or your "man of the night" because of any reason, don't do it. I don't care how much he begs, barks, or rubs his ding-a-ling against your booty—don't do it! Don't do it! Don't do it! It's a trap. If you are horny, go home and get some sexually enhanced oil for females, a sex toy and get it popping. Don't be afraid to make yourself feel good, Mama (hey, it's the safe way to go)! If you don't give up your cookies and masturbate you will wake up feeling better because A) you didn't give him any, B) because you got off, and C) because you woke up with no regrets (because if you don't take my advice and give him some anyway you will wake up feeling really stupid). Just think like this, a loser is not worthy of getting some of your catbag.

A MAN WHO DOESN'T WORK, DOESN'T EAT

Another thing that you better start saying no to quick are these men who are looking for a woman just to trick off of. Trick, you know as in get money from. Yes this fuckery is still alive and kicking and it's time to stop this stuff for real. Men who trick off of a woman are not real men but little boys looking for a mommy. Yes, it's the men who ask women to pay their car note, their cell phone, buy them jackets, or buy them shoes. Man, the list can go on and on and on. Don't get me wrong, there is nothing wrong with a woman being able to hold down the household, but first you have to have a household with this man. I'm talking about your beau who don't do anything else but beg, I'm talking about you helping a man pay his car note while your ass is taking the bus or you paying his cell phone and he doesn't even call you on a frequent basis. I know you just like to help out, but don't feel sorry for any man, because a man who doesn't make enough money for his own bills doesn't feel sorry for himself. And like my Grandma always said, "A man who doesn't work, doesn't eat," and it's straight up like that. I know it's hard not to help someone you love when they're lost and down, but who is going to support you when you need it? He sure as hell isn't, he can't even pay his own bills.

THE MONEY TRAP

The sad thing is you probably don't even know you're being used because his game is so tight. Girl, before he even asks for money, he has planned it for you to become his personal no-fees ATM. He calls you and says he wants to spend some time with you. Spend time, which usually means you cook and he comes over to eat all the food that he didn't help pay for. After dinner, his next plan is to lay the sex down, yes, get you dictomized (hypnotized by the dick). He's whispering sweet nothings in your ear while he's on top of you laying down the pipe like there's no tomorrow. You're so happy and shocked because he's still there in the morning. You're smiling from ear to ear as you get dressed in the morning. You say to yourself, "We are finally getting somewhere." This is the moment he asks for $200 to get his car out of the shop. Isn't it always to get his car out of the shop? Chances are he doesn't need that car if it's always in the shop. You walked right into his trap. Of course you give him the money. Even though you a have a million other things you can use the money on. He got you, and got you good.

I'm sorry to tell you that the money trap is only part of some of these losers' tricks. Sometimes they take your money to pay off a problem they have with another girl that they can't get out of by pleading poverty. Instead of getting a job they hit you up. It's usually the weak, fat, and ug-mug girls that they prey on, but hey, they get it. Please don't be one of these girls!

If they are just getting the money for themselves it isn't to pay the bills or to help look for work, it is for sneakers or beers to chill with their boys. I know you "love" him and I'm sure you think he loves you too, but you need to learn how to say no, because money doesn't buy you love. He'll smile in your face all the while you say yes, yes, yes, but the first time you say "No, I don't have it," he'll be out the door, because you're nothing but a bank to him.

A real man doesn't subtract from his lady, he adds and multiplies. So say no to the ho and get one step closer to getting your mind right. This is not Halloween therefore you don't have to trick or treat.

When in love, you have to think smart. Love is not all about matters of the heart, but in the mind as well. Women who think smart win in love.

Don't Lose It All
for "I Love You"

Rule
#4

ow much do you crave to hear those three magic words, *I love you?* I know I do. It makes us feel on top of the world. A feeling similar to hearing your favorite song on the road while driving real fast. But you have to be careful and use judgment. The word *love* can be a gift and a curse. A gift when someone means it and you know it's real; a curse when some loser-bozo uses it to snag you in his trap. Men will use the word *love* against you. If he knows he can get whatever from you just by saying it—he will say it; trust me!

YOU HAVE TO STOP BELIEVING IN FAIRY TALES

Movies, television, books, gossip magazines, even the Internet influence our perception of the meaning of love. How many times have you watched a romantic movie like *The Notebook* and thought, aww, I want to feel just like that? It makes some of us creamy when we hear a man say he loves a woman on television. Hell, we sit and imagine it's us who he is saying he loves (but he's not). You can watch these movies all you want, but trust me girl, your man is nobody's prince charming. He knows that if he pretends to love you, he can have you open like a token because all you want in the world is to be loved. This is why I think you should shut your mouth and not bring your daddy issues or stories of abandonment inside of your relationship, because he's listening and learning how to play on that. You're confused about love if you say the oh-so popular phrase "I know he loves me, but . . .". When you say this you're confused and making an excuse for all his indiscretions. It is not effing okay for him to do you dirty just because he says he love you or acts like he loves you. Don't allow yourself to be all caught up in those meaning-less words—seriously! Let your man's actions do the talking, not his useless verbiage.

We must remember that love is great when it's real but can be a distraction and destroy when it's a bunch of fuckery. Losing it all in the name of love is equivalent to being a sucker for love. A sucker for love is the type of person who would do anything just to feel loved. It's the type of woman who just doesn't care about anything or anyone the day her man is acting right. People who suffer from the "sucker for love" disease are just pitiful and you, my friend, do not want to be that person under any circum-stances. These chicks would sell their own mama out just for a man's affection. It doesn't matter what the man does, like a sucker, she's back up smiling in his face waiting for him to pat her on her ass.

The women I know who lose it all because of love many times settle in their relationship because they are afraid the man wouldn't "love" them anymore if they spoke up for them-selves. She makes her man her priority and puts him wayyyyyyy over anything else and provides his wants and forgets about her own needs. That's a bad mistake, honey! These women lose their morals, their goals, and their say on what's in or out (their control) in their own relationship. I am telling you, you really better stop losing it all for love, because what's left when all is lost? Yes, what do you have once he decides that he no longer loves you and wants to love another? And if love doesn't take over your mind, it will take over your well-being—your well-being in terms of how you take care of yourself.

DON'T GO ALL TO HELL JUST BECAUSE YOU FOUND LOVE

Many women get a man and they get sloppy-moppy: yes, fat, nasty, and just plain sloppy. There isn't anything wrong with gaining a little bit of weight during a relationship, but don't be like me when I was in my previous relationship and gained fifty pounds. Hell, I was always thick but after that relationship I was goddamn big. Yes, you can say it . . . that was just plain old ridiculous. Ladies, don't gain weight and eat up everything in the fridge just because you're in love and no longer looking for Mr. Right. That greed will turn your man off and you'll end up looking for a man again; just this time you will be a lot heavier.

The rule is, if he met you and you were a size 5, you must remain a size 5 throughout the relationship. If he met you and you were a size 14, you'd better stay a size 14. Keep your weight together no matter what. I don't care how many times a week you two go out to eat; you'd better add some cardio to that regimen and keep it right and tight. Don't become a sloppy-moppy, no matter what. This also goes for the ladies who get unsexy during the years or months of their relationship.

Some ladies get nasty and stop taking care of themselves. There are even some women who stop taking regular showers because they are so damn in love. Being happy doesn't stop the fish market from needing to be cleaned. Yes, stop being lazy and do that laundry. Girl, when is the last time you got your hair done? You used to get your hair done a lot before you got all fat and comfortable with your man. These men are already potential flight cases, don't give them an excuse to do you dirty. Stay hot so that if he plays himself, you can go out there and do him.

STAY SEXY

When he first starting sexing you, you wore those little things he liked. Now he can't get you to wear a see-thru thong if he puts a gun to your head. That is a huge problem with a capital P for many women. I know you heard this quote before, but it's very true; what you don't do, another chick will happily and willingly. I'd hate for you to lose your man because you got lazy and lost a piece of yourself. It's funny we want to lose it all for love and end up not taking care of ourselves, then get mad when our man looks at the next chick. Don't get mad at her because she looks good. Get mad at yourself because you made the choice to be a hot-ass mess. No matter if it is your second date or your sixtieth anniversary, you got to keep stepping up your game. If you want to keep the man, you damn sure better keep the sexy.

GIRLS WHO LOSE IT ALL NEVER WIN
IN RELATIONSHIPS

I know a lot of women who just go coo-coo for Cocoa Puffs when they meet a new guy. It's like you hear your friend went on a date and the next thing you know she is telling you how madly in love she is with the guy. When I hear this, I just want to smack the hell out of the girl, but I just listen. Then you have your friends who are just not happy in their lives unless they have a man to go home to. I often wonder, how do they live without a man in their lives? You have to remember that no matter what, the man is not your Jesus.

Men do not like nor do they respect emotional women. That's why it's very important not to say you love a man too quickly. I don't care if you do love him; try your best not to say it so fast because that is what your man expects you to do. He expects you to say you love him because that's what women do best. The woman who doesn't show the same regard toward him will be the woman he goes after most. Remember, men love women who play hard to get, no matter what they say.

There is nothing worse than telling a man who doesn't have a love bone in his body that you love him. The sad thing is his trifling ass will say it back even though he doesn't mean it because he's afraid to hurt your feelings. If you hold off from being the first to say the words, it will show him that you're not like all the other women that are beasting for his affection. He will see that you are a girl who doesn't wear her heart on her sleeve. The word *love* changes a lot of things in your relationship whether you believe it or not.

DON'T BE A VICTIM OF LOVE

You should never become a victim of love whether you think you love the person or not. Love is something that's supposed to uplift your relationship, not bring it down. You are the problem if you need to hear the word *love* all day just to believe someone cares greatly about you. One thing we all can agree on is that it takes maturity to really love someone, and also, we can't love anyone until we truly love and take care of ourselves. So ladies, get your mind right and stop falling victim to love. Take back your lives and emotions; better yet, let's stop saying the word in general until we are 100 percent sure we really mean it and that he feels the same way.

What my good friends former NBA basketball player Doug Christie and his beautiful wife, Jackie, have taught me is that love is infinite. Meaning you must love that person no matter what happens; you can't just turn it on or off. When I look back at the men in my past that I thought I loved, I didn't. I know now that I loved them in a friendship sort of way. When you're young and dealing with a man, you think you love everybody, but you just don't. You can love a person in so many ways; don't close your mind up to just one feeling. Take the time to explore your emotions with each person so you can know where every person stands in your love life.

It's great to talk, talk, talk to your man but if you really want to know how he feels about you, the best thing to do is listen, listen, listen.

Know Your Place
in a Man's World

Rule
#5

Many of us think we know how much our man cares about us and where we stand in his life, but we just know what he tells us. And as you have already heard me say many times: men will tell us anything just "to get in them drawers." But it is easy to get at this mystery and it is necessary information for you to have.

THE HOLIDAY GUT CHECK

If your man never invites you to any of his family gatherings or bothers to show up at your family's events during the holidays, then chances are he isn't really feeling you. You are more likely to be a jumpoff for him; yes, just a piece of behind. A woman he just has around for the bump and grind and not the long and winding road. It is hard to admit when we are a jumpoff, but we have to keep it real with ourselves and not color in a relationship that isn't there.

If you are a man's real lady he will want to bring you to his family's house for Thanksgiving and Christmas and every other holiday that comes along. A good man who is into you wouldn't miss being with you on important holidays. Family means the most to a man around holidays and if you're his woman, you're definitely his family. When a man doesn't want to spend the holidays with you it means that he has a woman already and she is not you. If you are uncertain where you stand, just give him the "Holiday Test": "Hey honey, I want you to come to Grandma's house with me on Christmas." And don't give him a way to get slick by saying Christmas morning or Christmas evening—don't give his ass any designated time because men are slick; he'll spend Christmas morning with his woman and their children and try to scoot on over in the evening to spend the rest of the evening with you. So don't give him any times just say Christmas. If he seems a little aloof or silent after your request, then chances are he is trying to figure out a way to tell you no without hurting your feelings, come up with a way to spend Christmas with all his ladies, or he's thinking about what his real girlfriend is going to think if he misses spending Christmas with her.

I know mad chicks that settle for their man not spending the holiday with them and they don't know that they might as well consider themselves as his mistress, because if he's not spending his holiday with you, he's spending it with his real girlfriend, and you can bet your rent money on that. I don't understand nor do I condone women who claim they have a man yet be the lonely one at Thanksgiving dinner every year. Women, we have to get our self-esteem game up and stop falling for the okie doke, and get rid of any man who refuses to spend the holidays with us or even buy a small gift on Valentine's Day. And while we're on the subject of Valentine's Day, I want to know why men make buying a gift such a big deal. Sure, some of us want Louis Vuitton bags or computers as gifts, but most women appreciate the little things in life like flowers, candy, and nice cards. Is it really that serious for a man to be so cheap on Valentine's Day that he'd break a woman's heart just to not get her anything? See, that's the problem when you're dealing with losers and bozos. A man who breaks up with a girl right before Valentine's Day just so he won't have to buy her a present is the ultimate loser. I can't believe that trick still works.

Ladies, don't forget about birthdays either. If your man doesn't spend time with you, and I mean quality time with you, on your birthday, he doesn't care about you, straight up. He knows that birthdays are important to you, he just doesn't care. He doesn't understand that his time is sometimes just enough to make your day great. Don't allow him to not show up on your birthday and then sit there and smile in your face the next day asking for some ass. If you let him get away with this, his respect for you will go down the toilet from there.

YOU CAN'T FORCE HIM TO MAKE YOU IMPORTANT IN HIS LIFE

I have always strived to make all my relationships from work to family feel special. My goal has always been to make myself a valuable person and to have a real connection to whoever it is in my life. But after dating for many years I realized I can't force a man to make me a priority in his life. He has to feel it for himself and make it his business to show me just that. Many women fail in love and relationships because they feel as if they can make a man feel a certain way for them. We think that we can make him want to hang out with us because we're cool; we pretend we love sports, and we give good head, but we're sadly mistaken. You can't force him to feel that way; he just has to feel that way.

You may have been important to other guys in your past, but that doesn't mean you're important to the guy you're boning now. Don't get mad because he doesn't treat you the way he treats the busted girl he's also messing with. Dating has taught me that a man could have a big, juicy sirloin steak on his plate in front of him but still beast for the left-over franks on the stove. That right there should teach you how to love yourself more and be real with your place in his world. Remember it's his world, so we can't judge or question his reasoning for doing things. All we can do is make sure we don't play the role we don't want to play.

Knowing your role is very important in any kind of relationship. I don't condone any woman being a mistress or recommend it, but I do think it's time for women to know their goddamn role and stop trying to mess up another woman's life once your role as the side whore doesn't work out. Some ladies love being the side chick, but once the man decides to place his woman or wife over them, they try to get crazy. No ma'am, don't get mad and try to mess up her life by calling her to tell her what her man did with you just because he stopped returning your phone calls or stopped paying your bills. You knew the risk you were taking when you decided to be the side chick and now you must live with that decision. The appetizer isn't usually as fulfilling as the entrée, so don't get mad, just move on and become a filling dish for another man. I am tired of women trying to mess up other women's lives just because things didn't work out. Calling the next chick will just make you look stupid because she's not going to leave her man just to let you have him. In these shitty situations, know your role and shut your mouth. If he thought you were important, he would have made you his woman and not just bone you at his convenience. Telling his woman what's going on isn't right, because another woman's pain should never be where you get your joy from. We are all women at the end of the day and if we stick together, we can and will gain back our power in relationships.

This advice also goes to the women who are in a relationship with a man who doesn't say how he feels about you, or he tells you but his actions are not adding up to his words. That's a big problem. You should never have to question your situation if you are in a loving and monogamous relationship. Questioning yourself will only confuse you and make you unhappy. Don't sit and wonder about what's going on; go to your man and find out what the heck is going on. You owe it to yourself to know exactly where he stands.

A MAN TREATS YOU THE WAY YOU TREAT YOURSELF

If you treat yourself with some importance, he will treat you as important in return. A man will only do unto you what you allow him to do, so if you allow him to miss spending a holiday with you, you better believe he will treat you like shit going forward. You can't give these men an inch, because they will take an effing mile. So ladies, remember if you're not his everything, you might as well be nothing to him, because sadly, your position on the totem pole will not change. The way you start will indeed be the way you finish. How many times do you have to touch the stove to know that it's hot?

Whether it's spending holidays with you or treating you like the queen you deserve to be, a man is not worthy of you if he doesn't make you his all and show you that you are the most important person in his life. It is a man's responsibility to treat you well and to do everything he needs to do to make you happy; that's it—case closed. If you are sitting there after years of being in a relationship and still wondering what your place is in his life, then you might as well consider the relationship as over, done. Always remember, if you're not first in your man's world, you're last, and that's a spot you should never aspire to.

You really can't get into a relationship until you get yourself together first. A lot of times we make the mistake of going from relationship to relationship and then we don't understand why all of them end up failing. Take the time to get yourself together if you plan on having everlasting love.

Chill with
the Baggage

Rule
#6

*I*t's time for women to say enough is enough and stop carrying around past years' loneliness and despair. For years I thought every man I met was the one with the problem and if they couldn't handle my *ish* it just proved me right. But boy I was wrong. I was carrying serious baggage. The Louis Vuitton of baggage. And it wasn't until I was ready to stop blaming others and see what I was dragging that I could move on and have a productive relationship with someone else.

When you have baggage from the past all you think about is what happened before. You find yourself holding back your love and not giving out many opportunities for love because you have been hurt before. It's hard to move on from turbulent relationships, and especially when we were dealing with a manipulative mind fucker, but we must move on and embrace love; because if we don't, the loser wins and a loser should never be a winner. We sit home and diss every guy who try to holla at us while he's on Wife Number Two. Men know something that we ladies are just starting to learn, and that's there is someone for everyone and if you miss one, another one is coming in about fifteen minutes.

GET OVER THE ISH

I have no time for women who take out baggage on someone else; the oh-he-hurt-me-so-I'm-going-to-hurt-you type of person. I know your mama taught you that two wrongs do not make a right. And it's not like you're getting revenge on the one who has done you wrong; you're taking it out on a new person who doesn't have any idea what happened in your past. That person may take the backhanded abuse, but seriously, how long you think that *ish* is going to last before he too picks up and leaves you? No one wants to be around miserable people, much less be dating a miserable person. You will always lose if you have displaced anger. That's why it's vital to get over the *ish* before you jump on the relationship bandwagon; *ish* meaning resentment, *ish* meaning hatred, *ish* meaning regret.

BAGGAGE ALSO MEANS
THE FEELINGS FOR AN EX

Ladies, you can't move on to a new relationship unless your brain and your booty are truly over your ex. This is one of the biggest mistakes women make when trying to pursue or start a new relationship. Some of us ladies are still stuck in the past with the fella we left a long time ago. You can't stay stuck dreaming about what you used to have. Forget the past; it's time for the future. Exes are exes for a reason. It doesn't matter whose fault it was for the breakup; so get over it! Many women allow their feelings for their ex to get in the way of being in a new, happy, and successful relationship. There is no going back and if you do you be back in the same situation that you were in when you left him the first time. There's nothing to think about when it comes down to an ex.

Do not be the woman who tricks herself into being single so she can be available when her ex is ready to come back. He most likely isn't coming back, and if he did—you really don't want him anyway. I have been there and have done that and believe me, it wasn't easy and it hurt my ego a lot, but eventually I moved on. After my ex, I wasted so many days thinking about him that if I had placed that same energy into getting myself together and opening up my heart to receive another—I would have been okay a lot sooner. Sometimes we can't get over our exes because we're too stuck in the past. We think over and over about what it could have been and should have been. As women we have lots of hope—hope that a bad situation for us would miraculously turn good, but it usually doesn't, so don't waste your time or the usage of your mind on a ex!

WHEN IT'S OVER, IT'S OVER

I am now happy that I didn't get back with my ex-boyfriend because it would have been a freaking disaster. There was nothing left to salvage in the relationship but memories. Girlfriend, take it from me: when it's over, it's over; there is no going back. You've got to get this in your brain while going through a massive breakup. I know it's scary to discover the unknown and to get back in the dating field, but you have to do what you have to do if you plan on being happy in the long run. Just think like this: if he really wants you back, he's going to do anything in his power to get you back. A real man knows when he's lost a jewel and he will come back to recapture his love under any circumstance. It's not the lady's job to try to make fate happen unless the problems in the relationship were undeniably her fault.

With every rule of love, there's an exception. You have some couples that broke up and have undisclosed things they could have worked out; those situations are different from what I'm talking about right now. In those cases, I think you can walk backward, but remember the man must feel like this is something that can be worked out as well, because it takes two to make things all right. Sometimes as optimistic women, we see things working out and our ex man doesn't quite see it that way. Ooh baby, how messy is that? That is why I am telling you that if he hasn't pursued trying to get you back, you don't go for it. Sorry! You don't want to end up being the one with pie stuck on your face.

Real talk: it's like this, we all have a soft spot for people from the past, but we can't let those feelings take over our futures. Sometimes you just have to let go and just move on and you never know—you'll probably meet someone better. And don't say no, there is no one better because you don't know until you are ready to meet someone new.

It is time to throw away the trash. Don't act like those old ladies whose apartments are filled with newspapers and junk mail because they are afraid of throwing out something important. You have to know how to decipher the junk, and exes, my dear, are the junk. Think about why you two broke up in the first place and come to terms with it. Okay, he cheated . . . okay, I cheated . . . okay, and we had communication issues. Stop being in denial with your situation! And if you are still in love with your ex and you guys decided to be "friends," it's time to stop being his friend—period. If you're still in love you can't keep being his Facebook friend, his MySpace friend, or his Twitter friend. Being able to access his life like that will only drive you nuts.

YOU CAN'T BE FRIENDS

Many people think that it's a good idea to be friends with their exes but it really isn't healthy mentally if you still have feelings for him. Being friends is just an excuse to continue to have him in your life. And if you're not friends with him, stop trying to be friends with his family and/or his friends too. Yes, so many women suffer from this. They try to act like they love his mama so much and you may indeed like her, but you don't need to visit her ass every single week. That's just plain ridiculous. My new motto is if you break up with him, you break up with everything associated with him. This is for your own sanity. I don't know, maybe you keep running over to his mama's house in hopes that you would run into him, which, as I found out the hard way, is very lame. Maybe you want his moms to ally with you so you can one day get back his love, but just know that's still her son and she may sit there and snap, crackle, and pop with you but really, she's no friend of yours. She sits and be friends with almost all the women he brings over there who break their necks to still be involved. And don't be the dummy that brings over some food or gifts when you come. Oh, his mother will definitely be like, shut the door bitch, come on in.

Think like this: so what if Mom is reporting back to her son about how good you look; how could he miss you when he always gets a live, secondhand update about what's going on with you? But that isn't even the point. If you guys are not together, you cannot be all up on his family; it makes you look weak and desperate.

DO WHAT'S RIGHT WHEN YOU ARE ON THE ROAD
TO GETTING YOUR MIND RIGHT

Don't put yourself in any position that will make you feel worse than you already are. You can't focus on *you* and move on with the good life if you're still stuck on what Ray-Ray is doing. Amen. Maybe in another life, you and he will be together forever, but right now you're not and won't be able to get it all together until you grow some hair on your coochie and woman up. Realize that was then and this is the new you. And the new you is baggage free.

Once a cheater,
always a cheater.

A Man Who Lies Is
a Man Who Cheats

Rule

#7

First off, let's clear up a lot of myths that you may have about cheating. Not only fat and ugly women get cheated on; men cheat on pretty girls too, and the sad thing is they cheat with uglier women. Hell, look at Halle Berry! She's been cheated on more times than a little bit and she is one of the most beautiful women on the planet! We have to be mindful that having great looks doesn't stop these fools from cheating on you. Secondly, it doesn't matter if you do everything sexually for your man, if he's a dog and he wants to cheat, he will cheat.

WHEN YOU ARE STARTING OUT, THERE IS NO SUCH THING AS CHEATING

Now I have a few theories when it comes down to cheating and I know that some of you are going to read this and think that I am totally out of my mind; hear me out though. For one, when you're dating, there's no such thing as cheating because you're not in a stable relationship. So what you have is a guy that you mostly see; you are allowed to date and make love to anyone you choose to as long as it's safe and consensual.

Many women and some men feel that when you're dating them, seeing another person on the side is off-limits. I think that's a whole crock of bullcrap. Dating is not definitive; dating is like tasting the sample before you decide to buy (which is marriage). Now if you're in a relationship (meaning you two guys dated and now you've both made the adult decision to be committed to one another) that's another story, but I still say that that's not your husband, so he still doesn't have any hand-cuffs on the booty, you feel me?

THE TRUST AND COMMITMENT CONVERSATION

As you all know, communication is an important factor to any relationship. You should have the talk before you two become exclusive in a relationship. I like to call it the trust and commit-ment conversation. In case you don't know what the talk is, the talk is laying down the rules and regulations of the relationship. That's the time when you and your mate discuss boundaries and mutual expectations. You need to talk about what cheating is, because the meaning of cheating is different to different people. To you, cheating may be your man having a conversation with the opposite sex on the phone or flirting with that receptionist at his job. To him, cheating may be you still having a friendship with your ex or just plain making friends with guys you meet on the train. See, you won't know how your man views things until you have that talk. Some people believe that even your thoughts can be considered cheating, but I say if that's the case, we're all some cheaters and going straight to hell on a fast train.

Getting your mind right is partly about being in touch with reality—your reality. I know we like to act all innocent, but let's face it ladies, sometimes we're bigger whores than men. Some of the best cheaters I have come across in my life have been women. They cheat hard bodied and their man doesn't even have a clue. That's not good, Ms. Bad Girl. We women are just better cheaters than men, because we're better liars than men. Men get caught up in their double lifestyle because they get sloppy while they're out doing their dirt. The best thing about when women cheat is if we cheat, there's a reason for it; with men, they cheat just to cheat (I guess they don't have anything else better to do).

ONE WORD OF ADVICE

When a real lady does her dirt, it's not with the average Joe from the same street corner our man frequents. That's word of advice for you young women out there; you never lay where you stay. Whatever you do out there in them streets, you make sure you do it discreetly, because as women all we have is our name, and your name must stay squeaky clean.

Men are just so thirsty for a little bit of coochie these days that it's not even funny; they could give two shits about where the next chick lives. They'll mess with the girl that lives downstairs from you—please, if he's really a horny dog, he'll mess with that busted bitch that lives next door.

ONE OF THE BAD THINGS
ABOUT MEN IS THEIR MOUTH

Contrary to popular belief, men are bigger talkers than women; yes they talk more than us. They talk to the next chick when they're in a messed-up situation. This is, in my opinion, the worse part about a cheater: when they go and sing about your ass to the side chick. They're yapping their mouths and then they wonder how they got caught when they're out there doing their dirt.

I want to stress this to everyone who is reading this: running your mouth to the next person about your lover or even your ex is the worse thing that you can possibly do. It is not classy and it makes you look bad. If a man runs his mouth to you about her, don't get hyped, just know that that is something he is going to do to you once you two aren't dealing with each other. Ladies, it is never a good idea to allow a man to assassinate another woman's character and I think any man who does that is a little biotch. Sorry, but I do.

I remember when my ex-boyfriend and I broke up and he got a new chick. He gave her a breakdown about my life year by year. He told her everything from how I was moving out of my apartment to who was knocked up in my family. I mean, he just disclosed too much information. If that's not some real girly stuff, then I don't know what is. Ooh, thinking about that makes my skin crawl, because that is so wack.

It's not good to hold things against people, but that right there made me real reluctant to tell another man anything about my personal business. So honestly, if your man is a singer, meaning someone that likes to go run his mouth, you better watch him.

AND IF YOU DO CHEAT, DON'T GET SLOPPY

Sloppy is when your man comes home with lip gloss on his collar, open condom wrappers in his pants pockets, and text messages in his phone that's blowing up spots. Your man should respect you enough to never get too damn sloppy with the next broad. The men that get sloppy just don't give a hoot-nanny about your feelings and what you find out because they don't care about the consequences of their actions.

At times, men can become so careless that they will text message (yes, sexting too) the next chick right from their cell phones. They are also taking nasty pictures with the next chick and saving it to their phone. The funny thing is, it is so easy to get caught up with these new "smart" phones. Yes, you better watch your man if he's really into technology. Man, the Black-berry gives you too many ways to get your freak on with the next chick (BBM, e-mail, AIM, etc.) Man, technology is the cause for many breakups these days; it will get you all caught up, so if you plan on getting a booty call, be smart and don't do it through your phone, period.

THE SLIP/UNINTENDED SEX

Cheating is not when your man goes to the bar after a very long and stressful day of work, gets drunk, and has sex with the woman on the next stool. That's a slip. And while he is a dick for doing it, because no matter how many drinks he had he should have been able to think about the relationship that he already was involved with, it was still unintended sex. There were no emotional ties and he most likely doesn't even know the girl's name much less how she worked it. I'm not saying it is right, but at least it's unintended. Let me explain, because I can guess you are not nodding along with me here.

He did not go to the bar looking to give up his sausage, he just got caught up in the moment, and to me, that is forgivable. Hopefully, he will stop drinking because he doesn't know how to hold his liquor if he's boning chicks that he barely knows. Now there's a big problem when your man cheats and the next chick thinks she's his main chick. That right there is a hot mess and not forgivable under any circumstance. I never was a victim of my man cheating on me (meaning if he did I never knew), but I was a victim of being the next chick, not knowing this dude had a situation on the side, and when you find out it's devastating. Whether you're the real girlfriend or the side girlfriend, it's a big mess, and both of you women are the victims.

The sad truth here is that it will never end if you both don't leave him alone. Like my situation with the other woman, we were both strong minded and believed that he cared about us and we both kept going on. Thankfully, after a long and tiresome struggle, finally I decided to let his filthy ass go.

CHEATING IS ALL ABOUT THE EMOTIONAL CONNECTION, NOT THE PHYSICAL

Your man needs his behind kicked if he has a side piece and he bought her the same diamond tennis bracelet he bought you. It is not forgivable that he has had this woman for just about the same time he has you. Now, this is a case of a man who just doesn't give a damn; this is a person who you should get a first-class ticket away from immediately. He is a slimeball type of person and he has no respect for you and women in general. This is a dangerous man, a man who just wants to have his cake and eat it too, and you, my dear, need to watch out.

He doesn't care about your sanity; all he cares about is himself. If he's tricking on her like he's doing on you, he's really feeling this chick. Don't let him bamboozle you into thinking that she's nobody, because he's a goddamned liar, he loves this girl and he doesn't care what the outcome of this situation is as long as he's with one of you ladies. It's even worse when the next chick knows about you. Boy, that's real crazy. If none of these things have ever happened to you, go right now and bend down and praise the Lord, because you, my dear, are truly blessed; but if it did happen to you, figure out a way to never let it happen to you again.

HOW TO RECOGNIZE THE SIGNS

There are usually signs when your man or the man you think is yours is cheating on you or has a woman; signs that the denial in our hearts won't allow for us to see. I always preach that one of the best qualities a woman possesses is her intuition. Our intuition is one of the best friends we can have and we must really pay attention to what she says to us. Our intuition tells us the story straight up and down whether we want to hear it or not.

If you've never been to his house or never had his house number or address, chances are he has a girl. If it seems like he's only disclosing a small amount of information about himself and he's acting all secretive, go with your first gut, he probably has a woman who he is already shacked up with. If he barely calls you, does not introduce to you to anyone close to him, or does not like to be seen in public with you—chances are he probably has a girl. You gotta wake up and smell the coffee while it's still perking! Don't be afraid to question things when in fact you see the signs! If he doesn't like questions, then he doesn't like you, because a smart woman will always ask the questions that she wants the answers to.

I really don't want you to waste your time if your guy is acting all sneaky, but I know you will, because as women we need the absolute proof before we can walk away. We barely ever walk away when we first hear stuff or when we become suspicious. We wait until the little blaze turns into a huge, uncontrollable fire.

IT ALL COMES DOWN TO SETTLING

When you accept a man cheating on you, you have to ask yourself, are you in love with this man or are you in love with the point of being in love? Do you just want a man to impress your friends or your family? It all comes down to settling. I understand that nobody wants to be alone, but that should not be the reason why you just sit there and take the bullcrap that these men are dishing out. We must be real with ourselves, we're living in terrible times where it's too dangerous to be sleeping with a man who sleeps around with a whole bunch of chicks. That's what made me stop messing with that fool who kept going back and forth with his baby mama. I didn't have time to be messing with some loser and thinking about whether or not I will wake up with an STD. I'd rather play with my vibrator or resort back to Mr. Showerhead than deal with a man that's running around on me. There are too many diseases and infections out there these days that you can get even while using a condom. Thank God I have a real man in my life now, because baby . . .

Ladies, I can't stress enough how important it is for you to protect yourself and get you and your partner tested, because men that cheat carry a lot of baggage with them and you don't need to be the one suffering in the end. Just sit back and imagine all the nasty things you and him do in the bed. Now think about him doing that with someone else.

*In life you never want to have
to deal with regret so treat
the one you love accordingly.
One woman's trash is another
woman's treasure so be good
to the one who is being
good to you!*

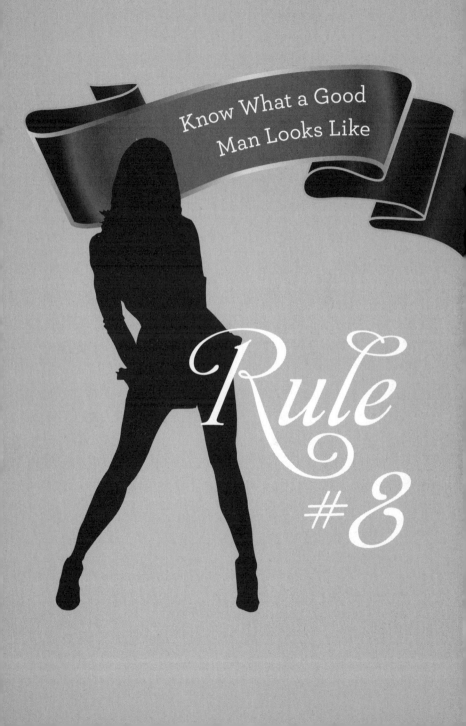

Know What a Good
Man Looks Like

Rule
#8

Many of us are guilty of failing to notice a good man even when he is right in front of our face. There are still some very good men out there in the world; you just have to be lucky enough to run into them. I know from personal experience it can be hard to believe that there are good ones still out there, but it really is just a matter of getting your mind right and you will meet your man.

A GOOD MAN IS HARD TO FIND

A good man is hard to find because you are not always looking in the right place. He's the guy who is always willing to give you a helping hand or your homeboy who is always there for you no matter what. Sure, he may be a little dorky or a little overweight, but he is the man who would sell his left testicle just to be in your presence, and that, my friend, is the person you need around. He's always there when you call and he puts no one before you, not even his own girlfriend (who he's getting coochie from). You think he likes you but you're not really sure, so you brush it off not realizing that this man does more for you than your last three boyfriends combined. Ouch, that is a harsh reality, but it's one you must acknowledge if you plan on finding Mr. Right.

Once you get your mind right, you will realize that the man who does everything for you and is always at your beck and call is possibly the man your ass needs to give a chance to. I'm not saying go have sex with your homeboys who look out for you because those friendship lines usually should never be crossed, but I am saying look at the signs, homegirl, because he is right in your face. He sees something in you that John, David, and Chris didn't, and he's ready to love you for you. He sees what you see in yourself, because he's taken the time to get to know you—something that most men do not do. He listens to your complaints about your exes and he secretly dreams about the day when he can show you better. He drops little hints like, "Hey, lets get something to eat!" and you take him up on his offer but your mission statement still is "Never gonna happen, buddy." After a while he realizes it's never going to happen, so he decides to give up and remain a friend or helping hand.

Why not give this man a chance? He's the only one there for you through thick and thin, and to be honest, that's what is missing in relationships these days—riding (someone who sticks it out with you no matter what). They are there for you when you're up and they are there for you when you're down and they never treat you any differently. One day you may be a superstar to the world and the next day a broke little girl from the hood. Either way his love doesn't change for you and his goal is to still make you happy under any circumstances.

LOVE THE MAN WHO CARES FOR YOU

We women complain a lot about the shortage of men, but we never think about the ones who ride for us and do even the little things for us like shovel our car out of the snow (he's your neighbor, he doesn't have to do that for you) or the guy who helps because he is giving you a chance. Introduce your world to those who want to be in your world and not the ones you have to force to go to Sunday dinner at Mama's house. Having a man who wants to be there by your side is your goal because it's not about who's around, it's about who *wants* to be around. When was the last time you knew that a man wanted to be around you with no hesitations? Just around you and your being? So ladies, cut the crap and love the one who loves you! Stop chasing someone who doesn't care about you no matter what you try to do to woo him over. Love the one who loves you.

BE WITH THE GUY WHO IS INTERESTED IN YOU MORE THAN YOU ARE INTERESTED IN HIM

Stop caring about the guys who don't give you respect and start checking for the guys who are checking for you. I know it should be mutual, but honey, you're fooling yourself believing that two people can be into each other at the same pace. There's always going to be one in the relationship who is more interested in the other and usually when the man is more interested it seems to work out. That's why I don't want any of my ladies going out there trying to find a man. Let him find you and when he does find you, you will know that it's right. You deserve to be the object of a man's affection. You don't need to be the one hunting him down, trying to make him feel a certain way about you.

CORNY MAY JUST BE WHAT
THE DOCTOR ORDERED

I know sometimes it seems as if the ones who are head over heels for us are wack or corny, but sometimes to stop the love triangles, you have to deal with a square. It's just the way real life works. I am tired of women always talking about how someone is corny. You have to stop yourself and think about that when you say that, because it's crazy. The woman who always goes after the "popping" guys will always be left stranded, because every woman is going after that same goal.

It's really time for you to make life easier on yourself and enjoy being enjoyed. It's time for you to stop being so uptight and give someone you normally wouldn't a try. Yes, ladies give the mailman a try or the man with a dream a try. Start looking at the ones who just think you are the best thing since sliced bread, because they are the ones who will adore you most. It feels good to be loved and adored, and I think if you notice a good man and give a few more a try, you will GET the man of your dreams.

W.W.A.M

Sometimes you have to believe in what I call W.W.A.M (Work With A Man). Yes ladies, sometimes you will meet a guy who doesn't quite meet your standards, but you have to work with him if he does demonstrate potential. We women are so quick to just throw someone good away that we don't take the time to wait for a man to get it together. Sometimes if you want the "perfect" man, you have to help create the perfect man. I know working with a man can of course backfire in your face, because you wait on him or help him get it together and he can turn around and diss you, but I am hoping this doesn't happen to you. If he is a good man, this won't happen to you.

Being with a good man these days who's not jumping out on you or otherwise disrespecting is truly a blessing, because the men out here nowadays are so freaking reckless. You can't go anywhere in public (the beauty salon, the bus, the doctor's office) without hearing a woman complain about her no-good man, and it is sickening. That's why you have to thank the heavens for the peace you have in your own relationship if you are one of those women who already have a good man in her life but don't appreciate him.

DON'T IGNORE THE MAN LYING RIGHT NEXT TO YOU

There are a lot of single women out here that pray and cry to God every night in search of a good man. Baby, they will give their nipple up just to have a good man hold them down at night. You better get up, get sexy, shut the hell up, and stop complaining, because girlfriend, you have a good man on your hands. If your man treats you well, sexes you well, comes home at night, and handles his business like a man—he's a good man. He's a good man who could have a thousand women on his Johnsons if he wanted to do so. A man with less could have a hundred women chasing after him, so you know what the deal is. I know you like to look at yourself like you're hot and he can't get better, but baby, I am telling you—you better get right and you better do it right now.

A man who doesn't bring you home any problems is a man who genuinely loves and cares for you and your feelings and it's time for you to recognize that. He's a beautiful specimen whose only job is to make you happy. Women all over the world envy and salute you for having him the way you do, so why do you insist on putting this brother down?

Girl, you better learn how to treat that man because one day you might find yourself by yourself; looking and feeling stupid over the great man you lost. I could see you now, going on dates with other men and feeling like someone who has a big L on her face all because you couldn't take a second to appreciate the good man you once had. I can bet you that most women reading this book will take that good man off of your hands with no problem, so you better get your mind right and appreciate the fact that you have a good one.

Seriously, learn how to shut the hell up and appreciate a great guy when you have him the way you want him. Stop complaining about the little things that happen in your relationship. Does he make you happy? Does he make you smile? If he does, love him the way I know you can, because your love is important to him.

MEN LOVE THE LITTLE THINGS
JUST AS MUCH AS WE WOMEN DO

You should never sweat him too much because for some men that *ish* goes straight to their heads, but always show little initiatives that let him know that you're into him; like buy him something small that he's been talking about and don't ever forget the little things when it comes to making your man happy. Make sure you keep doing the little sexy things he likes, like going down or doing a striptease dance for him. Always stay freaky and make sure you listen to him and his dreams, because some of us women (especially me) have a problem with listening.

These days you better do whatever it is you have to do to keep your man happy, because there is always another chick lurking and waiting for your leftovers. I am not saying that doing all of these things will prevent him from going astray, because let's face it, men are greedy, but it will show your appreciation for a man who has been good anyway. Having a good man is a beautiful thing and I would hate for you or myself to lose him because we're not on our game.

No matter how good-looking another chick may look, remember that she doesn't have anything on you. Beauty is in the eye of the beholder and you are what you think you are. Don't let anyone else tell you that you are not beautiful.

Stop Comparing
Yourself to Her

Rule
#9

Many women compare their happiness in their relationship with other people's relationships and that is a problem. Making comparisons to other relationships or how other people live will just leave you sad and jealous. Also, you have no idea what is really going on in other people's homes behind closed doors. Hell, she could be getting her ass kicked behind closed doors, he could be cheating, and she could be burning from a nasty STD. Who knows and who cares? It's not good to compare yourself with others because it makes you look stupid. Instead of fixating on how great someone else's relationship is, take a moment to be with your man to discuss what your likes and dislikes are. It's not a sin to look at others and learn, but when you sit there and hate and then get mad at your man because he doesn't do the same thing her man does for her, you're leading yourself to destruction. Eventually your man will leave as it is impossible for any human being to live up to your conception of what a real couple should do.

THERE IS NO SUCH THING AS
A PERFECT RELATIONSHIP

You may feel that all your friends are in better relationships than you as they are always telling you about all the good things their man has done for them. And the only time you get to hear the bad things is when they have a huge argument and no one else answered their phone. That's when you will hear how he was talking to someone at his job and she forgave him and how he makes no money and she wishes that he made more. "Um, it was all good a week ago" are the words that keep replaying over and over in your head. "Where the hell was I when all of this was happening?" you say to your damsel-in-distress friend, but she just ignores the question. See, things happen in every relationship. Maybe your man doesn't hug you the way her man hugs her. So freaking what, but your man damn sure ain't doing the dirt her man is doing on her either. Lighten up and stop sweating what she has going on. While you are looking at what is going on in her relationship, you're not enjoying the things that are going good in your relationship. You have to focus on why you started liking the fella in the first place.

Relationship rubbernecking is not the only things that we woman are guilty of. We compare our money, bodies, and gear to the next chick. Every woman has their own style. Sure, we may look at some other woman and think that she's a bum, but hey, what is a bum? And while you're sitting there thinking she has no sense of style, someone else is sitting there thinking the same thing about your ass. Some women dress expensively, some don't. Some women have nice jackets, some don't.

KNOW YOUR WAVE

While it is important to have your own style, it's equally healthy to know your wave, meaning know what you are capable of doing and what you are capable of handling. The best example I can give is when you go shopping with someone who is a self-diagnosed shopaholic. You went to the mall knowing that all you needed was a black dress, but you came out with bags filled with stuff just because you saw her do it. I know your mama taught you better; be a leader, not a follower. I don't care how much stuff homegirl was buying. That doesn't have anything to do with you. I don't care how much pressure she was putting you under; you should never shop on impulse. Now you can't eat lunch for the rest of the week because you wanted to be like her.

I am also sick of people who try to get overly competitive on you just because you are out there grinding, making your money. We have all had a friend who changed the amount of money she made every time she heard about the amount of money you made. When you were working at McDonald's in high school and making $5.15 an hour, she worked at the Gap and made $7.75 an hour. Now the high-school days are over; you both are working at two very good firms. You slipped up and told her you made $50,000 a year and you remember her telling you she made $45,000 when you were out there looking for a job and asked her what her job was paying. All of a sudden you got this new promising job and she tells you she is now making $65,000. You're thinking, wow, she got a $15,000 raise in the matter of months, but no, that's not the case. She's just doing what fake-ass, phony people, also known as your frenemies, do—LYING. I think this kind of person is the saddest because they can't accept being defeated and you find out later (after she stops speaking to you because you're now on such a level that she can no longer compete) that she was full of crap. She was surely missing out on her blessing because she was too busy trying to see what you had going on. If she would have placed half the energy on herself that she placed on you, she would be quite all right, but now she's just a loser trying to find some other deadbeats she can appear to be doing better than.

There's always someone who seems to have better and you can't be that chick until you can accept this fact. I don't compare myself to any other person, because in my mind no one is fucking with me regardless, and that is the attitude you must have if you plan on being that bitch. Sure, I have stretch marks, cellulite, and am fifty pounds overweight, but I love me and I know that my tongue is what makes me special. What is that thing that makes you special?

There is something special inside of you. Something that is too powerful to touch. You will be all right once you find and embrace it.

You Got That Thang

Rule
#10

onfidence is key when you are in a relationship and most of us just don't put enough of it out there. Good men are drawn to confident women and only loser men are looking for insecure women. The good news is that every woman has something that makes her sing. What really matters is how you see yourself in a world filled with buxom beauties and superficial values. How do you see yourself when you wake up and look at yourself in the mirror? Do you see anything that bothers you? Do you ever wake up feeling like you wish you were someone else? I hope not, but if you do that's your business. It's really time to change your self-image. A new car doesn't make you who you are because a fly girl could drive a Hyundai and make it look like an S-Class Benz. I know you hear this a lot, but it's not looks that make a man treat you like you're that chick, it's the swag and the way you carry yourself. If you treat yourself good, he will treat you good and that's just it.

THE WAY YOU TREAT YOURSELF IS
THE WAY HE WILL TREAT YOU

Have you ever seen an unattractive young lady walking down the street with a fly-ass man? He's tall, dark, and handsome with swagger for days, and she is just what we call "blah." You see the way he is looking at his queen and the way she is just allowing him to lust in her presence and you say to yourself, "That's one ugly girl. How is that possible?"

You feel bad for calling another woman ugly, but you just can't help yourself because all of your life you thought that fine women were the only ones a man treated like royalty. But you're wrong, sister. In fact, less-attractive women get treated better than attractive women. And although you may think that appearance is everything—it's not. He likes her not only because she can cook and suck a mean one (our assumptions on why ugly women get good-looking guys), but because she thinks she fly, therefore he in return believes in that very same notion. Remember, the way you treat yourself is the way a man will treat you. If you treat yourself good and don't accept any bullcrap, he will treat you the same way because it's only right.

When you get older and go through different experiences with men you realize that looks don't matter. I think men realized that a long time ago, because the most overweight, cross-eyed, bowlegged man in the world will step to you with the utmost confidence, and most of the time they end up getting your number and you don't know how in the hell that happened. It happened because you looked past his looks and loved the fact that he made you laugh and looked right into your eyes like he just knew he could have you. See, that right there is an example of confidence and how it could get you a long way. One day you're looking at this sweaty man like ugh, the next he's up in those drawers. It's definitely time for us women to get our thoughts about ourselves and the way we handle men together. I am tired of pretty women thinking that they can keep their man because they are pretty. Step your game up and get it together, period. Having confidence will save you from a lot of headache later down the line, because once you know what it is you want and are confident that you can get it, you will succeed in love.

YOU CAN'T SIT AROUND AND EXPECT A GUY TO TELL YOU HE LOVES YOU ALL DAY

You can't look into that guy to make your ass feel better about you. Women who depend on a man's love for the love they are missing within will end up alone and lonely. The main ingredient that's missing from one getting their mind right is self-esteem. Having self-esteem will prevent you from going through most if not all the bullcrap that you go through. Women who don't have self-esteem accept whatever it is that is thrown to them because no matter what they may say, they really don't think they can do better. And if they know they can do better they don't think that someone better is going to want their ass. I know that sometimes we stay with an effed-up guy because A) we're afraid to be alone and B) we're afraid of the unknown; but where do you think that fear comes from, young lady?

The fear comes from the lack of belief you have in yourself. You need to acquire confidence, and I'm talking about real confidence, confidence so great that no one could tell you nothing. You're not going to tolerate anyone coming at you in a disrespectful way, let alone a man cheating on you. Why do that when there's another man out there waiting and anticipating your love? You're not going to think that way if you're too busy being unconfident about the things you don't have going right—

my legs, my waistline, my teeth (although I recommend that you take good care of those).

Confidence is about looking at the good things about yourself and making it work for you. And even if you're not a total Betty, at least you love yourself enough to know that you don't have to take nobody's mess. I also say have self-esteem because a man knows when you don't and will play with that very same fact. My line about men has always been, men play different women in different ways. And that's a quote you should always remember because it's the truth. So with that being said, a man will always fuck over women who don't love themselves. Believe that, honey bunches of oats. In the beginning he'll pretend like he's trying to build you up, but what he's really trying to do is figure out how far he can go with you. If your self-esteem is not too low, he'll try you, but not go overboard. But if you are sunk in depths of insecurity you might as well change your name to "Doormat," because there will be a lot of walking over your ass going on. Trust me: he will barely call you (because he can do that). He will barely take you out and he'll only claim you as his woman when it's convenient for him. Convenient as in when he needs something from you like money, sex, or company.

WHAT ARE YOUR BEST FEATURES?

Start writing down the things that you don't like about yourself and change those things one by one. You hate your hair (cut it), you hate that your legs rub together (lose the Crisco between them), and you hate the city you live in (get your ass up and move). It is straight like that. Only you can make the changes you need in order to get your self-esteem up. Trust me, once you make those changes you're going to feel really good. Then you are definitely not going to take no mess. Also, if you know there's something about yourself that you don't like, don't tell anyone. Just get it together! Complaining about yourself shows a man—a person, period—your weakness and once someone knows your weakness they can take over you and your soul.

KNOW WHAT MAKES YOU SEXY

Looks do not matter if you have confidence as every woman has that thing. And while there really aren't any ugly people on earth, hey, we all know that there are some HAMS (hot-ass messes) out there in the world. But don't sleep, my dear; even those HAMS could get your man. Many times we diss our friends who don't look as good as us, but it's really time to start giving them their props because every woman got that thang. The difference between the ugly and the cute ones is that the ugly ones know they can bag a man and go hard doing so and the cute ones just sit around and wait for him to approach her. I see many unattractive girls getting it in the club and having a great time because beauty is only skin deep and what we as women feel is unattractive may be just what the doctor ordered when it comes down to a man. Men have the wonderful ability to pick out the best things in a woman. They be like, oh, she's not the best-looking girl, but the way she smiles is infectious. I give them mad props for this. We women could learn from their being able to see beauty despite what others say.

KNOW WHAT MAKES YOU SEXY

You need to know what it is that makes you sexy, because every woman has something that makes them feel sexy and makes them feel better than ever. For some women, it's their hair. They love their hair. They have been wearing the same hairstyle for twenty years and they don't care what anyone says because the first thing a man mentions when he's trying to court her is how pretty her hair is. She knows that she is turning heads once she walks into a room because her hair is sexy. For other women, like me, it's their boobs. They know if they wear a tight shirt, they're shutting the party down because there's no tatas quite like those tatas. Then it's the booty, the legs, the smile, and the attitude. If you're one of those lucky women, you may have multiple things that stand out, but there's always one thing that outweighs everything else. Once you figure out what that thing is, you need to know how to work it. Remember it isn't about showing skin or jumping up on the boys. You need to let your strut speak for itself.

One of life's biggest misconceptions is that attractive women know that they are attractive. Well I say that's a bunch of bullshit because plenty of attractive people get played and go right back to the bullcrap. I think they're not aware of the fact that they too could do better. Some women are more concerned with their looks than their inner strength and their being as a woman in general. Don't be one of those ladies. . . . It's pathetic and very sad. Being good-looking won't stop you from getting played. Knowing that you are too much of a good woman to accept bullshit will. Lots of times, your unattractive friend is stronger than you are mentally. Sure she may have to work harder than you, but so what? She got the man and most of the times you don't. I laugh at the way women joke on other women not realizing that this chick that is so busted has more going on for herself than they do because she knows what she has to bring to the table and they don't. They have that comfort in themselves, which sets them apart from others. Many pretty people always sit around discussing their imperfections. They have no comfort in themselves and no matter what it looks like on the outside, they really don't love themselves in the inside.

Confidence will help you find what makes you sexy on the outside and give you "inner sexy" that will set you apart from all other ladies. Men are drawn to that inner-sexy glow, so go get your shine on.

The way you treat yourself is the way a man will treat you; so always treat yourself good, because believe me, he's watching!

Attitude Is
Everything!

Rule
#11

en are often intimidated by good-looking women. They would rather jump after bummy chicks they think they can make over than go after the super together woman. The make-a-chick syndrome. Yes, as much as men preach about how they hate chicks who aren't doing it for themselves, they love a bum chick. They love to make a chick over and teach her things he thinks she doesn't know anything about. Like the rapper Biggie Smalls said, "You were a Reebok Chick but now you're wearing Chanel sandals. I made you why would I play you?" Yep, they love taking a chick on the next level because then that's their power over you. Men like the busted ones because they think that the busted ones will love them forever.

Men think it will be too expensive or take too much effort to go after a super with-it girl. They feel like, Damn, I am never going to be able to make her happy. Look at how many things she already has; I can't help her. Or even if they could afford her lifestyle, they still have some kind of distrust, because she has the power to just get up and find her own way. But you should not give an inch on this one. You just have to find a good man who can play at your level.

It's similar to like how they feel about girls who talk a lot. They think that women who talk a lot are more promiscuous than those who don't. Men who think this way are sadly mistaken as quiet girls are the biggest whores.

CONCEIT NOT MISTAKEN FOR CONFIDENCE

You should never, ever settle for a loser man, but don't mistake conceit for confidence. There's nothing wrong with loving who you are, but do not let that turn you into a cocky asshole. There are lots of women who are pretty like supermodels, but they are alone because their attitudes stink or their images of what a man should have are too out-of-this-world. These types of women are what I call delusional. These are the women who over and over again truly believe that their shit don't stink and that there's no man on this earth who is worth their time. They may play with a man every now and then, but they are always looking sideways for a more perfect man.

There isn't anything wrong with trying to find a good man (although a good man will find you) and there isn't anything wrong with a woman with standards, but don't block your blessing just because the man's jeans don't fit him right or because he eats too many potato chips. Your tendency to diss men is just you blocking your heart and they are immature. You will never find the right one by doing this bullshit. We all know a woman who swears she's the bomb, yet her ass never got a date. Oh, you think it's a coincidence or the luck of the draw. No way, chances are she's alone not because she wants to be, but because no good man in his right mind wants to date her wacked attitude.

ATTITUDE IS EVERYTHING

Attitude may be the very thing that is keeping you away from finding the right guy. If you constantly lose men and don't know why, chances are you're the problem. Have you ever sat yourself down and asked yourself, "Is it me?" Well if you didn't, here are the questions you should ask so that you can get your mind right and your attitude on the right path:

1. Is it me? (Does the way you carry yourself scare men away?)

2. Do I talk a lot about myself on the first date and never ask about what's going on with him? (I know this may be weird coming from me, but men hate women who talk too much about themselves.)

3. Do I brag? (Lots of girls who got it talk a lot about how much they make or the kind of car they drive. They brag about their money, then wonder why they attract nothing but money-mooching men looking for someone to take care of 'em.)

4. Do I shut him down too quickly before giving him a chance? (Many confident women shut down a brother before even considering their situation. I was guilty of this very same thing back in my single days. Sometimes you just have to give people a chance.)

5. Am I too judgmental? (Often we judge our potential suitors because they handle things differently than we do. A man never wants to be around a woman who he feels doesn't like how he acts.)

There are many questions you can ask yourself, but these five are the most important ones because these are the main things "attitude-y" women are guilty of. All these bad habits are sins of love and are not good for those who want to be in long-lasting relationships. As I admitted earlier, I was guilty of all those effing things because I didn't know any better, but that's why I am sharing the good word. If you knew better, you'd do better. So start analyzing yourself more so you can have it all together.

Girl, get your mind right and be true to you. Yes, you're fly and yes, the perfect man for you is out there, but you have to do things right so everything can be all right. Have confidence— know to walk away when something isn't right, but most of all, do not let your cocky nature take over your love life.

Never accept disrespect in your relationship because once you do you are opening a door headed nowhere. Whenever something is going ill in your relationship, speak up! No one should stop you from expressing your opinion. Don't just sit there and accept him running wild in front of you. Love yourself enough to say, "Hell no, I am not having that."

Be a Bitch if
You Want To

Rule
#12

Many women suffer from nice girl-*itis*. The sickness that makes a woman feel like she's supposed to be nice in order to keep her man. Every woman has suffered from this plague, but I am telling you, *eff that ish*. Nice girls finish last and get taken advantage of like it's nobody's business. I am tired of seeing women be nice to the wrong kind of guy. Yes, there are some men you should play nicey-nice with, but most of them you should just be the witch that you are. A lot of times men take women's niceness for weakness—and I am not saying we don't think the same thing of men, but right now it's not about them, it's about us. And sometimes being the "It's okay, baby" type of woman isn't healthy or helpful for our relationships or lack thereof. Sometimes a man needs to know that you mean business and that you don't play that way. Some situations are very serious and need to be handled accordingly. Don't smile and give him the puppy eyes when you catch him doing the dirt.

WHEN TO PULL THE WITCH CARD

1. He told you that he was going to call and you have been waiting on that call to figure out your own plans, but he never did.

    Not only is he not feeling you, but he needs to know that you don't play that way. First off, you don't call his ass back, and when he finally does call you, you kindly let him know that you are not the girl that he should be igging (ignoring). You tell him to have a nice life and hang up the phone, because time is money. And you don't call him no what how much it hurts. He will get the message and either get his act together or you will see that he does not want to be your man.

2. You go out for a romantic dinner, but he acts like a clown and ignores you.

Bad enough he didn't pull out your chair like a gentleman, but he sits there and texts all damn date long. A chick like me would have asked him to stop texting right away, but you're a nice girl and you want to give a dude a chance. You try to be sweet and ask him nicely to pay attention to you and not the phone. But he doesn't get it. So know you have to act. You finish your food (because you never waste free food) and you exit left because this date is clearly over. It's not being bad, it's being good because no one has to sit there and accept a man not paying attention to you. Obviously the person or people (depending on how much of a whore he is) he's texting are more important to him than you are, so don't waste your time—get the hell out of there. Texting at dinner is a no-no. It's very effing rude and you too may be guilty of doing it, and if you are, you better stop because it's not cute. Facebook, MySpace, and Twitter are included. You don't do that on a date. Save the charm for the one on your arm.

3. Your man is still friends with his ex, who would sell her left tit to get back with him.

Oh, hells no. He knows this chick likes him, yet he is still calling her and possibly hanging out. Do not accept that bullshit, because if it's not messy now, it will be messy later and I would hate to say I told you so. You need to be a witch regarding this situation as this is a problem with a capital P. Eventually this young lady is going to cross the line. It'd be a different situation if homegirl didn't still have feelings for him, but she does and you know a woman: we won't stop at anything to get exactly what we want. She will pretend as if she's just giving him a shoulder to lean on when times get bad, but really she is just sitting there trying to find out what it is that you are doing wrong as his lady. I say don't play that *ish*. Stop the bullcrap before it begins. You let him know that you are not comfortable with him being all happy-go-lucky with his ex. No, he's not supposed to hate his ex because then that's some extra baggage your ass shouldn't have to deal with, but he should keep her at bay and just be cordial.

4. He's spending more time with his homies than with you. He should be boning his boys if he wants to spend more time with them than he does with you.

If he's a man and he's in a relationship with you, he has to know his limits. First of all, what kind of friends does your man have? Are his friends players? Because you already know that birds of a feather flock together. Just like they say, if you hang out with a bunch of hoes, you may be a ho. It's the same thing for a man. If he's happy and his friends are not, they will try to get him involved with some fuckery, but they can't do that unless he allows them to. Now, you want him to go with you to your home-girl's birthday party, yet he says, "I'm going to chill with the boys." You let him rock because maybe he doesn't want to cramp your style while you are hanging with your homies. Then you ask him to hang out with you and watch a movie in the house and have a weekend of you-and-him time and he still opts out just to hang out with the boys. Oh no, sister mo, don't even let that happen. There is a problem if he doesn't want to chill with you and wants to chill with them. You can give him wayyyyyy more than his friends can, so he needs to under-stand that. You let him know that you're not having it and tell him why he needs to spend time with you versus them. If he still chooses the boys, you let his ass go hang out with them, but he needs to know that you too have other important things to do and won't be sitting there waiting for him to get his mind right, you have better things to do. Believe me, he will change his tune mad quick on this one. That's being a witch! A righteous witch. Girlfriend, you can't change the fact that he wants to chill with his friends, that is his choice. But you change the way you handle the situation.

You are not a pony, so don't allow a man to take you for a ride. Men know a weak woman when they see one, so make sure you are always armored with strength because you do not want to be a victim. Love is not worth it if you have to pay for it. Remember, you can satisfy yourself for free.

There Is No Prize for
Dating a Broke Man

Rule

#13

I have dated my share of men, honey, and one thing for sure—two things for certain—nothing is worse than dating a broke man. Broke men prey on independent, well-to-do women like yourself because they are looking for a mama. Yes, you read it right: a mama. One who can take them into their arms and just feed and burp the little broke baby. They want to be taken care of rather than working to get their own money, because they know women are so damn desperate these days that they will trick real quick on a man without any hesitations.

IF HE DOESN'T BUY THE CEREAL
HE DOESN'T EAT BREAKFAST

I am not saying never take a chance on a man who is looking to improve himself. But a man has to work to show worth. He can't just move in on you and take over your house and home when he doesn't buy anything and doesn't pay any of the bills. That is an absolute no-no! No matter how far we come as women, we all want a man to do his job and help us out. Women are now making the same money as guys and sometimes more, but hey, something has to give. Hell, you have to pay the cost to be the boss and if you don't pay, you don't stay, and that's straight up. I want you to repeat that to yourself, especially if you made the ultimate sin and allowed a broke ass to live with you. Broke men don't feel sorry for themselves, so you, my friend, shouldn't either. You better learn real quick who's a loser and who isn't!

Being in a relationship with someone who is flat-out broke becomes very frustrating, very quickly. You can't go to dinner, you can't go away, you can't even feel good about buying yourself stuff. I once messed with a guy who was so broke that he didn't even have enough money to get on the train to come see me. I cut him off because a man that broke doesn't need pussy; he needs some integrity and a job application.

DATE MEN WHO ARE ON YOUR LEVEL

I know we all don't like to admit it when the person we love is not on our level. We kick, we scream, and we run away from the facts that are placed on the table in front of us. As women, we are always trying to get the impossible out of a man. It's great that you have faith in this man and really believe that he is going to be someone great in the future, but face it, you gave him a chance and he's a freaking loser. It's not your fault. He has that devil leaking inside of him and he just doesn't want to do right. He tries to get himself together but it just doesn't work.

YOU DON'T NEED A LIABILITY IN YOUR LIFE, YOU NEED ASSETS

A broke man is a definite liability. If you have a man that's a liability, get rid of his ass (quick). You can definitely do bad all by your goddamn self. Think about it like this: you have two jobs and your man doesn't have one, what do you need him for? See, everyone thinks like this, but they're too afraid to say it aloud. I believe in supporting your man's goals and all, but there's a difference between a goal and a goddamn dream. I'm saying if he never has anything to bring to the table, he has to go. I know chicks that allow these B.A.D. (Broke-Ass Dudes) to live with them and they always live to regret it.

Sometimes in life, you have to keep yourself entertained.

Bish, Get a Hobby!

Rule
#14

*I*t feels good when you fall in love. Your whole body and heart loses control and you really don't know what to do with yourself. Everything you do is about you and him, even when his ass isn't around. You and your girlfriends could be talking about a new jacket that's on sale at Saks Fifth Avenue and all of a sudden you say, "Oh Larry's sister got that jacket." You could be talking about something as simples as apples and you'll say, "Oh Larry's allergic to apples." Your friends would look at you like *bish*, did we ask you?

No matter how much a man loves you, he will never lose too much of himself in a relationship. Men keep their friends and they keep the things that they love to do around, no matter what. It's so crazy how much a woman gives to her relationship. I mean, your man reigns over everything and that includes family, friends, and the things you used to love to do. When I see women who suffer from this dysfunction, I wonder, did you ever have a life before you were in a relationship? Get a hobby and get one quick.

Yes, honey, a hobby, as in something you like to do besides hanging with a man, sexing a man, or thinking about a man. Ladies, I can't emphasize the importance of this enough. Even if you are in a loving relationship it is very important to have something of your own. A hobby could be anything from knitting, designing clothes, or collecting magazines, to going bowling and taking online classes. It's anything that you enjoy doing that takes up your time.

Many times in a relationship, women become so obsessed with their man—obsessed as in they can't stop calling, talking about, or thinking about. Suddenly they don't have any other interests besides him. Ask the average women what she enjoys doing in her spare time and she really can't answer you. . . . Ask her about her man and she can answer you in 0.6 seconds.

HAVE A LIFE OUTSIDE YOUR MAN

This is one of the best things you can do for yourself and for your relationship; and if you're not in a relationship, remember this advice and your relationship will last longer than your last one. See, women who don't have any hobbies or any friends are annoying to a man because they have too much time on their hands. That's why you call him so much—because you have nothing to do—and any wise woman knows that you never call a man too much because it makes you look desperate. Men lose interest in women who have nothing else to do—trust that. You could be at a Young Professionals or a Moms Who Like To Cook meet-up instead of sitting there constantly harassing him about his whereabouts.

Ask any man and he'll tell you he loves a woman who has a life of her own. Stop trying to hang out with him and his friends and get some of your own. If your man wants you around, he'll keep you around. Stop dissing your homegirls just to stay in the house up under his ass! This type of behavior will lead you down a road of destruction. You really have to find other interests.

Think of the things you like to do other than hang out with your boo and go from there. Women who are social don't stress having a man as much as women who don't have shit else to do. Ladies, it's time for you to do something besides going to work and calling your man.

THE MORE YOU DO THINGS YOU LOVE, THE LESS TIME YOU HAVE FOR DRAMA

By the time your man has the chance to hang out with you, he'll appreciate you even more. In case you're clueless about what a hobby is or what other things you can get involved with besides being canoodled with your man, your girl Tionna Smalls has your back. Here are ten suggestions for a great and productive life:

1. Volunteer at a homeless teen shelter—the girls would really appreciate your time and your wisdom.

2. Bake cookies for your local public school.

3. Join a league such as basketball, softball, or even kickball.

4. Find a meet-up group that interests you, such as Young Professionals.

5. Visit a lonely or elderly family member weekly and spend some quality TIME.

6. Take your children or nieces and nephews to the movie or the park.

7. Get some religion! Get something in your life you believe in other than him.

8. Have brunch with the girlfriends. Yes, nothing is better than sitting back, chilling with the ladies who make you smile the most.

9. Go on road trips. I don't care if it's two hours away. Get up and go, and girl, have some fun! Stop in the candy shop and have a Snickers bar.

10. Get in shape. Hit up the gym. It may become one of the best decisions you ever made.

These are only suggestions, but I wrote them so you don't have any excuses. Your world will definitely expand once you have something else to do besides him. Take the time to work on *you*, because you want do the things that keep you right. So girlfriend, get a hobby and trust me, your relationship will be ten times better. It's always good to have something to do. Like after-school programs are to at-risk youth, hobbies keep your butt out of trouble. So get a hobby and get one quick!

Don't ask someone for their opinion if you don't want to hear their true take on your situation. If you are a person who gets offended easily, keep your business to yourself, but let's see where that will take you.

Don't Lose
Your Friends!

Rule
#15

*I*t doesn't matter what you go through with your girls—it's important to realize that you need them (well, the real chicks that you have in your life anyway). No matter how well you think your relationship is going, one thing you better make sure you never do is diss your homegirls. I am sick and tired of females getting rid of their friends once they become obsessively involved in their man. I understand that things change when you are in a relationship, but it should never change so much that you lose touch with the people you know who have been there for you through thick and thin.

I'm not saying go out every day with your single friends because hey, you really can't go out every day when you are someone's woman, but try and take some time out to show your real homies your appreciation. Don't abandon them just because you're happy right now, because as you know from your past relationships, happiness doesn't always last long. And who would be there for you if you got rid of everyone in your world?

Like hobbies, you need something to do besides sweat your man. If friends are very important in your world, then your single friends should be something that's important when you're in a relationship. Don't ever get so busy in your "relationship" that you don't have time to pick up the phone to touch somebody.

A man is supposed to be more into you than you are into him. Remember ladies, it's very important to love the person who loves you!

You Can't Have
Sex Like a Man

Rule
#16

*S*ex is good. For some of us sex is great; however, no matter how far we have come along as independent women we still don't understand the dynamic of sex and our feelings. Many of us just don't know how to cum and keep it moving. We always want to feel like there's more once we have sex with a man, not realizing that the men that are having sex with us could care less. No matter how much of a player you think you are, you can't have sex like a man, because sooner or later, those emotions will take over.

I know a lot of women (including myself) who are proud of their sexual prowess, yet they still get caught up. It's not their fault, it's just about how we were all raised to believe that we should not have sex, and if we do, it should be when we are married or at least in a stable relationship. I guess the person who made up these social norms never thought about the fact that women outnumber men and everyone is just not going to find a man. With that being said, girl, you must never, ever, ever mistake sex for love.

MEN ARE DETACHED FROM THEIR DICKS

It's good to get your freak on, but it's time to stop thinking a man likes you or cares about you or loves you just because he has sex with you. I'm sorry, but I didn't make the rules, I just live by them. It's time to stop mistaking one good piece of bun-bun with love. Lots of time we have sex with a man and because he's kissing us and tasting what the catbag is cooking we think they love us. I know that when he's on top of you, that penis feels real good. I mean really good, but girl, don't fall for the old okie-doke. It's just your mind playing tricks on you and I'm here to save you from the embarrassment and the heartache.

It can be devastating to meet a guy and think he's into you, just to be duped. If you are woman enough to have sex, you have to be woman enough to know the difference between love and lust. It's very easy to become bamboozled or attached to the D when you're doing your thang, but you have to know when to stop yourself. The best thing to do when you're open off someone sexually but can't figure out how you feel about them mentally is to step back from the bedroom and really decipher the situation. It goes for the opposite situations too. You don't go from not really liking someone to then falling in love with them once the sexing happens. That is a real confusing scenario that you should really try to avoid. Don't allow sex to change your feelings for someone.

The men that we are giving so much up to are many times not into us. They bang us and it's really on to the next one (men move on so easily). We women are the ones who are crushed once the love affair is over. Sometimes you can sit in dead-ass denial, like, "Oh my God, but he came over almost every day. How could he not be into me?" He never told you that you were the only one, so don't assume that you are the only one! He didn't say a word and you too are guilty, because you never took the time to ask yourself if you were basing your emotions on what you wanted, which at the time was his sex.

YOU HAVE TO SEE BEYOND THE D

Men out here are sick and they'll take everything from you if you let them, but we can't really blame them because we are the ones with the catbag who are letting them. The sad thing is, we're giving up the goods and these guys barely make us feel good sexually, let alone special. Nowadays, men are not focused on making you satisfied; they are trying to get in where they fit and that's in between your legs. They are just worried about themselves, so be careful and don't get all emotional and caught up in the moment of lust.

There are women out here who think that once they have sex with a guy, that means that they control the guy, but they're wrong. So what you had sex with him? That doesn't mean he's your man. No your coochie isn't that good that once you bone him, you own him. Sorry Mama, but this is real life and it doesn't go that way. He doesn't have to answer to you, because you and him didn't have any commitment before sex, so do not ask for a commitment. He got his and hopefully you got yours, and this is not to discourage you, because if you're a big girl you're ready for big-girl things. You are welcome to submit yourself to booty call/jumpoff behavior. But most of us ladies are not built for that and need to stop fronting like we are.

NOT EVERY WOMAN IS BUILT TO GET THE SEX AND LEAVE THE MONEY ON THE DRESSER

Most of us just don't have it in us to just wash off the coochie and keep it moving. I tried to be like that for hot minute, but that playgirl lifestyle didn't last long, because after a while I wanted to be in control of the guy; I wanted him to hold, caress, and need me after, but it didn't happen. I broke the player's code by getting all caught up in the mix. The mix meaning I didn't follow the rules of knowing who to get intimate with and who to get in a relationship with. I broke the rules; I tried to turn a jumpoff into a hubby all because I liked how he sexed me. Shame on me and it will be shame on you too if you participate in this unhealthy behavior.

YOUR BODY IS YOUR TEMPLE
AND YOU ARE WHAT YOU BEAT

You have to be very cautious about who you allow inside your catbag. Sometimes we get so caught up on getting it on and popping that we don't even focus on who we are allowing inside of our bodies. We must really watch who we let in these days because when we have sex with someone we're actually feeling the inside of their souls. We must be careful about who we allow in our bed, because many of our partners carry spirits that we may not want to possess.

Have you ever started acting like the man (personality wise) that you were having sex with? Meaning you start saying the same things he says, watching the same kinds of movies, eating the same kinds of food. Sex is like that too. If you have sex with a depressed person, you find yourself feeling depressed too. All of this is the transferring spirits. The men puts it in us. Even more so without a condom. So beware of what you put in you. Too many dicks bring on too many personalities.

KNOW YOUR FEELINGS
AND ASK HIM ABOUT HIS

Being attached to the D is a good thing if and when you are in a healthy and stable relationship. It is extremely important to have communication with any person you are being intimate with just so you know where they stand. You can't have a happy, healthy relationship without this. Ladies, don't think that a great piece of ass is your guide to a happy and healthy life. It is very important to separate your true feelings from those you experience in bed.

As emotional people, it is very easy to get into someone you're banging who's not necessarily into you, so know what it is. Be careful of the men you have sex with and the spirits you pick up. Sometimes the best thing to do when you're lonely and emotional is to keep your panties up. Doing things this way will keep you from getting caught up and being an emotional wreck. Know the difference between a man that's fuck-able and a man that's keep-able, and you should be the winner at the end of the day. Remember, you have the vagina; therefore, you have the power.

A partner is supposed to be the better half of you and vice versa. Don't get into a relationship with a person who doesn't complement your fancy, meaning make you a better person. Don't bring losers in your life that will take away from you. Love is all about additions, not subtractions.

Leave the
Thugs Alone!

Rule
#17

I know a lot of women who are smart, beautiful, and well educated, yet they still choose to date all of the wrong men. Many women I know love thug fizzles, a.k.a. thugs, gangsters, gees, bad boys, rock stars, etc., because it turns them on. They make the excuse that it is just their preferences in men, but if you ever want to get your mind right, you have to get really serious about the men you choose to be in your life and get rid of all the bad boys in your life. Messing with a bad boy will be exciting for you in the beginning, but later on down the line it will affect your life in some kind of negative way.

Many of my good male friends (meaning those who are employed and good to their women) complain a lot about how nice guys finish last and this is the one debate that I often lose when discussing relationships with men. I lose the debate because in the end of the day, I do believe that often, nice guys do finish last. We women complain about how there aren't any real or good men around but go right on dissing the nice guys and jumping after the guys who walk with their pants hanging down and talk with a little bit of slang.

WE WOMEN LOVE
TO CREATE A MAN

I think most of us women like bad boys because we like projects: something that we can fix up and make better. Our little thug becomes our little pet project: we dress him, we feed him, and we teach him how not to take a dump on the couch (meaning shit where he lays). This exercise makes us women feel needed. In the end of the day, all women want to feel is needed and loved and that is what we believe he supplies to us.

The problem with creating a man, also known as (I like to say) "building a man," is that we lose a little bit of ourselves along the process. This man is grown; it was his mother's job to teach him the tricks of the trade and to teach him that there is more to life than being some thug.

THERE IS NO FUTURE
WITH THE BAD BOY

I don't know what it is about a tough guy, but we women just lose control when dealing with one. I know you feel secured when you're dealing with this so-called bad boy but you're wasting your time. I will tell you this up front: there is no future with a bad boy unless he ends up changing his ways. Bad boys bring nothing into your life but a lot of drama and you, my friend, don't need more drama in your life.

What you don't understand about most bad boys is that they live a very fast life and they have little to no time or interest for a relationship. I know his toughness turns you on and makes you feel protected, but that is a quick feeling that too will pass. Right now you're caught up in the whole fun of things, so naturally your mind is not working straight—so don't get crazy!

HE IS NOT GOING TO CHANGE

Like my Grandma always said, "You can't teach an old dog new tricks." Do not trick yourself into believing that your bad boy will one day change his ways and lifestyle just to be with you, because you are wrong. Honey, all the gushy coochie in the world isn't going to change that man. He has to change because he wants to change and in order to do that he has to see some kind of error in his ways. Sadly, most dudes who live destructive lifestyles do not see that they have a problem, therefore they do not change.

You have to understand that these bad boys are "bad" because they want to be bad. They like the fast life, the fast money, and the fast cars, but do you ever stop to think about what comes with the fast life? Huh? Yes a lot of things come with that fast life, like fast-ass girls who, like you, are attracted to bad boys and would stop at nothing to get their man. Other problems, such as being that ride-or-die chick when your man gets locked up or inheriting their problems on and off the street. It's a lot that comes with it; so you have to make the adult choice on whether you want to live that lifestyle with him or not. If you don't want to live that "hectic" lifestyle, you need to get out of that relationship ASAP!

YOUR BAD BOY CAN'T HELP YOUR FUTURE

We're living in tough financial times and things are getting really hard in the world. You will have a tough time building a world with your guy if you want to get married to this guy and build a future with him. These days you can't even get a proper apartment without good credit. Most bad boys and thugs don't have any real credit and no real savings, therefore they can't help you buy a house or anything else because of their unstable lifestyle. Unfortunately, street pharmacists don't get pay stubs.

Without a real paper trail he has nothing that he can possibly bring to the damn table except for his petty drama. Sure, he can buy a Louis Vuitton bag quicker than a guy with a real job, but think about the stress you are going to have to go through when the pursuit of fast money catches up with him. Ask any chick who dealt with a thug and she will tell you that it is hard being the hustler's wife. There's only so much riding or dying you can do before you get freaking aggravated and realize that it's not worth it.

I know you want to believe that he's working the block for your future together, but remember there are not many retired thugs. Your beau is only going one or two places: to jail or to the casket. There's not much else in between.

So what's wrong with these bad boys besides the lifestyle they lead? Well what's wrong with them is they don't think a lot about the future. They just think about what is popping right now, like the expensive luxury cars and designer shoes. That may be something you like, but think about how you will feel once you have learned that he doesn't think about his future as a husband either. I don't care if you are the chick that he was with before he became a "hood star." He thinks he's one of those rappers and wants to frequent the streets and deal with a whole bunch of women all while he is dealing with you. No one has time for that bullcrap.

CAN'T TAKE A THUG OR
BAD BOY SERIOUSLY

Your bad boy should just be there for one thing and that is for companionship, not for a relationship. You should never get too caught up in this guy; you have to know that this is fun and that's all it's going to ever be. You can go out clubbing, but don't try to bring him home to meet your parents and you damn sure don't ever, ever have children by him. Having children with this type of guy will be a massive mistake, the fact being that you don't know his future. You have to think about whether or not he will be around by the time the baby is born. It's just a little too much.

We females mess up when we start to believe in our own bullcrap. We are truly hopeless romantics. It seems as if we love everything that is bad for us. We love the chase, the adventure, the excitement, but we never see what's wrong with the picture because we want what we want (bottom line). Life would just be easier if we looked past our desires and focused on our priorities, which is our life (present and future).

Do you believe in Santa Clause? Because I don't! I also don't believe in the lies and the hopeless dreams that these bad boys try to sell to us. And I don't believe that if we make everything good for him (cook, clean, and ride for him) he will turn around and want to have the good sweet home life. Ladies, I don't want you to be with no punk guy who can't protect you from a fly or with a guy who will sit there and watch you get beat up; I would never recommend that for you. If you want to be happy in your life, you better settle down with a guy who works hard for his money (legally) and knows how to present himself. He needs to bring something to the table besides visits to jail and other dumb crap.

Bottom line: if you want to grow and get your mind right, you have to get rid of the loser and focus on a person who can help elevate you to the next level. You don't need to be baby-sitting this bad guy all because he's interested in you. Have fun and move on. Once you leave the thugs alone you will see how free your mind will become.

There are always more fishes in the sea. So don't settle for the one that can't fill you up!

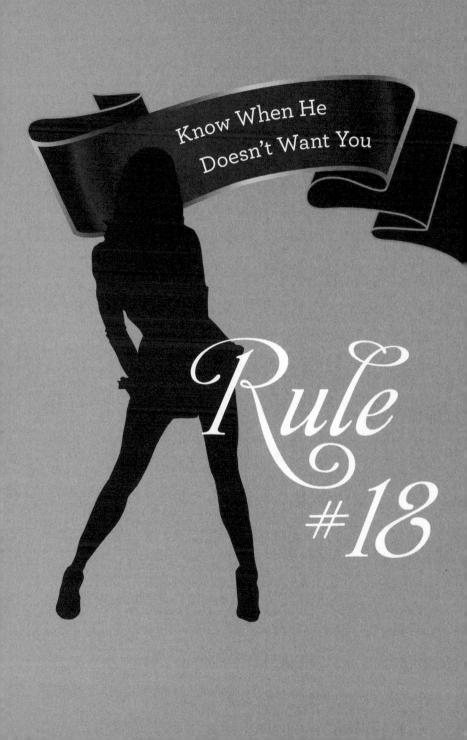

Know When He
Doesn't Want You

Rule
#18

We always discuss the men we have or had in our lifetime, but we often forget about the men we haven't been with or probably won't ever have. Yes, it's time to talk about the men who don't want you under any circumstances. To many of us, not being wanted is a very hard pill to swallow, but the older you get you realize that the inevitable will happen to you.

Don't roll your eyes while you read this chapter thinking that every man you ever wanted in your life wanted you back, because if you think this way you are in real and utter denial. Every woman, I don't care how beautiful you are, has been denied by a man before. Whether if it was when you walked by a guy ten times and he still didn't seem interested in knowing your tight booty in that even tighter mini skirt or you asked a guy for his number and he just kind of laughed it off. Those are examples of a man who just don't want your behind. Maybe he doesn't want you because he's already taken or he's not into skinny girls or he's not into fat girls—whatever the reason is, stop blaming it on him being gay.

It kills me how so many women will brand a man as gay just because he doesn't seem interested in pursuing a romantic or sexual relationship with them. It's like, come on now, you may be a good flavor, but you're just not going to be every man's cup of tea.

STOP GOING AFTER MEN
WHO DON'T WANT YOU!

We women have to stop going after men who don't want us or becoming upset with ourselves when we come across a man who rejects us. It seems like the more a man doesn't want us, the harder we go to get his attention. We're not realizing that we're making ourselves look cheap, dirty, and desperate, and nothing turns a man off more than a desperate woman. Check the scenario: you and your girls go to the club and y'all dancing and having a hell of a time and the next thing you know you see your "dream" guy. You walk by him hoping you can get his attention but it doesn't work. So you walk by him again hoping that you can get his attention this time around, but nothing. He keeps sipping his drink like he never saw you.

It doesn't mean you're unattractive just because you didn't get his attention.

All you did was attract some other dude who you didn't want to get attention from and since he saw you walk by not once but twice in your freak-em dress, he decides to follow you all night long. Great. . . . After shooing off the new stalker guy all night you leave the nightclub asking yourself, did you lose your mojo? And the answer is no, you didn't lose your mojo or your "it thing," you just didn't attract that man's attention.

A MAN HAVING A CONVERSATION WITH YOU
DOESN'T MEAN HE WANTS TO TAKE YOU HOME

Some things are just not meant to be. Maybe it wasn't meant for him to meet you that night in that way. Take a chill pill! That is just a missed connection. Let's get to some real gritty situations where a man may deny your advances. You meet a guy somewhere while out. You're having a great conversation. He's flowing with you and you're vibing with him. You feel sparks so you decide to be bold and ask him for a contact number. But he acts like he doesn't hear you and keeps on having the conversation. Only now the convo is getting a little more causal and he keep stating that, "You're mad cool!"

He's stating you're cool and you're thinking he's not, but you're still not understanding the key words that are coming out of his mouth. All you are doing is assuming that this sexy man is talking to you all day so he must want you. Ugh, Miss Thang, it doesn't take a genius to find out that he doesn't want you. You asked him for a contact number and he straight-up did the "deaf act" on you when he acted like he couldn't hear you. He did that because he really didn't want to hurt your feelings because he thinks you're cool.

LEARN HOW TO TAKE A HINT

I know it's hard but sometimes you gotta learn how to take a hint. If he wanted to continue the conversation, he would have been the one to ask you for your information. This is not always the case, but in most cases it is. So don't be so quick to get his information and let him get yours.

DOES HE REALLY WANT YOU, OR ARE YOU TOO AGGRESSIVE?

I used to be a very aggressive little bumble bee back in my single days, but I chilled with that over the years because I realized that I was meeting guys who hooked up with me only because I was sooo aggressive versus really wanting to be with me or getting to know me better. I'm not saying that I put a gun to their head or anything, but I did come on a little strong. It was like they were afraid of me or something. Afraid I would go in on them if they didn't give me what I wanted. I decided that I didn't want a man to kick it with me because I went hard. I wanted a man to kick it with me because he actually wanted to.

DON'T THROW YOURSELF ON A MAN

There are a lot of women who just sit there and throw themselves at men: married men, taken men, single men, toothless men, employed men, etc., etc. I truly believe that this is an example of having a self-esteem problem they incurred a long time ago. These women will literally throw their panties in a man's face and he is still not interested. They will attempt to perform oral sex on a man, show up to his house with no panties on. I mean the list could go on and on. This is some crazy *ish*. Lady, if the man wants you, like really wants you, you wouldn't have to go through all of that craziness, because he will come after you.

You have to have some pride in yourself as a woman and say no, not me. I am not going to play myself and throw myself on any man. If a man wants some of your sweetness, he has to come your way and court you.

HE NEEDS TO WANT YOU

A man wanting you more than you want him is the only way any man-woman love affair will work in the long term. Yes, Mama taught me that and it's a very true theory. When the woman wants the man more, her love is often taken for granted, so watch how you carry yourself even if you want something so bad.

And this goes for the man you have or you think you have now. Sometimes in relationships, things go wrong. You grow up and you grow apart. It comes to the point where there is no romance and he makes it evident that he doesn't like you or is not into you as much as he used to be. You have to take it for what it is. Stop trying to make lemonade if you don't have any lemons.

IF HE DOESN'T WANT YOU,
SOMEONE ELSE DOES

There are plenty of men in the world that will find you to be attractive, so don't waste your time on no loser who just isn't interested in you. We have to stop dancing and prancing around a man trying to get his attention, because when we do, it belittles our existence.

Sometimes you just have to take an L. Yes, take the loss and move on with your life because there are so many other men out there. When a man ignores you, don't dwell or get mad if he doesn't seem interested, because if he's not interested now, chances are he won't be interested later and all you're going to do is waste your time and you don't want to do that under any circumstances.

HE MAY HAVE WANTED YOU BEFORE,
BUT THAT DOESN'T MEAN HE WANTS YOU NOW

A lot of times, women stay with men who make it clear that he no longer wants to be in a relationship. He does this by cheating or by not having sex with you. I don't know if it's because you got sloppy over the years or it is because he has someone new, but the fact is he doesn't want you. Don't sit there and settle for that bullcrap because you guys have been together for so long. You should never sit there and be with a guy who makes it clear that he doesn't want you. It's something that can really mess up your self-esteem. You have to be strong enough to leave that situation if need to be, because in the end you will be hurt.

A man who does not want you will do anything to show you that he doesn't want you, including take your love for granted. He will do things with no remorse and you will sit there and take it because you love him. Don't love him more than he loves you. See the signs and take action, because there is a nice guy out there who is yearning for a little piece of you. Want yourself and make better decisions for yourself and your life.

Create the world you want to have and never settle for less!

Girl, You Have to Act the Act,
Not Just Read the Words

*C*ongratulations, you reached the last chapter of this book. Hopefully you found clues that will take help you on the path to getting your mind right. And I mean totally right. But, girl, know that the road doesn't get any easier from here.

You need to know that even though I believe in every word in this book, it is not a magic potion. You have to act the act, not just read the words. So take what you can from here and listen to yourself, believe in yourself, and lead yourself to the promised land of love.

It's always easier said than done. I encourage you to try your hardest to make changes in your life. But the change starts with you. Things will never change in your love life until you decide to change it. Everybody around you is tired of seeing you go through the drama, but nothing will be done until you get tired of it, and honey, I want you to be tired right now.

Getting it together means you have to make the right decisions when it comes down to your life. Yes, meaning you have to think with your mind and not your heart. You must always listen to your mind when you meet someone because your mind will never disappoint you. You need to turn your intuition so when you meet someone new you will know if he is a loser or a good man.

You are getting yourself ready for Mr. Right. Finding him or receiving him is not easy—if it was, everyone would have him—but remember nothing in life worth having is. And being ready for Mr. Right and for happiness means getting your mind right. Happiness is different to different people. Maybe your happiness is finding a man to touch you in the morning, but for other women it may be spending time with a good man or experiencing infinite love, which is the love that is owed to you. Whatever it is girl, be ready! Be ready to get rid of everything and everyone that is making you go left. You can't have your mind going left when you're trying to go right!

I wrote this book because I wanted you to know that you are not alone. I didn't always use the brain that God gave me and that my parents birthed to me. I just went out and did whatever it was that I wanted to do, all willy-nilly. After I realized where my actions were taking me, I decided that I wanted to be free. Free from all the losers and utter a-holes.

Sometimes you have to take a step back from yourself and watch every woman around you and how they deal with themselves and a man, and trust me, you will learn something. I know I have learned over the years and I am happy that I made the conscious decision to get it right, and as soon as I got it right I met my man. Yes, I had to hump a lot of frogs to get this prince, but I got him and now I am woman enough to appreciate him.

Girl, Get Your Mind Right! is not just a title; it's a demand. You have to get your mind right for yourself and for all the little girls in the world around you who are watching and looking to you to learn the game. Believe it or not, they are watching and it's our duty as women to show them how to play the game of love and life. Remember, a woman is precious and one of the best gifts of life, so with that being said, know that you are a prize to a man and not the other way around. It doesn't matter if you consider yourself as ugly, pretty, fat, or skinny; the rules don't change.

Love is a game and I hope after reading this book, you win the game and receive a fulfilling reward and not one of temperament. Believe me, change takes time. Just remember there aren't mistakes, just learning experiences and you're good as long as you learned a valuable lesson.

I would like to thank you for reading this book. I want you to pass it along to every woman you think needs the advice and let the Girl, Get Your Mind Right! campaign begin. I love you and pray that you allow the love you have for yourself to conquer all. Welcome to your new life!

Congratulations, my sister. Peace and blessings, Tionna.

*And remember
change in relationships
starts with you.*

1. **NEVER "DUPE" YOURSELF.** When you sit there and let a guy do you dirty, you're basically signing your strength away, and therefore, you're duping yourself. Remember that a man only does what you allow him to do to you.

2. **STAY STRONG EVEN IF IT MEANS BEING ALONE.** Yes, it's true, no one wants to be alone, but if a man is doing you wrong, you're alone anyway. Being strong is the beginning of a healthy life and relationship. Remember that a man doesn't define who you are.

3. **DON'T FALL VICTIM TO THE PENIS.** Yeah, we all want it, but how much are you willing to risk just to have it? I know it feels good but don't risk your life for fifteen minutes of pleasure (if you're lucky). I know he has some good stuff, but don't let him do you wrong just because you're horny. Read a book, take a shower, and get over it!

4. **REMEMBER TO FORGIVE, BUT NEVER FORGET.** In order to move on and have a great life, you must let go of all the hurt and the pain you endured in the past. Moving on will free you from lots of stress and make you more of a fierce chick. There is no such thing as regrets, just learning experiences. Remember that and you will go far.

5. **ALWAYS KEEP YOURSELF TOGETHER.** I don't care if you only got $2.00 in your purse, you better keep yourself together and always have your best foot forward. Looking good is one step to living a happy and healthy life. It's true that when you look good, you feel good and that's what it's all about, especially if you are trying to get that Mr. Right! Men are attracted to women who take care of themselves.

6. **ALWAYS STAY POSITIVE.** I don't care about how bad your situation is, you must believe that it is always going to get better. Positive people are successful people and successful people are positive people. Remember that if you think good thoughts, good things will happen to you, and that's something we all strive for. Surround yourself with nothing but positive things, and I guarantee that you will feel like a better person.

7. **REMEMBER THAT IN THE END, ALL YOU HAVE IS YOURSELF.** Don't ever depend on someone else to make you happy mentally, physically, emotionally, and financially; always depend on yourself. I don't care how many people you think you have in your corner when times are bad, remember that when the smoke clears, all you have is you. There is not one person in the world who is going to jump in the casket with you when you die. Try your hardest to live your life for yourself. It's a great feeling when you have someone to lean on, but you must understand that that same trust you have in that person as a support system is the same trust you must have for yourself, no matter what.

8. **BROADEN YOUR HORIZONS.** You must go out and experience new things if you plan on getting your mind right. Maybe you're meeting all the wrong men because you're closing yourself in one box and not welcoming other great prospects to come into your life. Go and do something you have never done before and watch how quickly your life will change.

9. **DON'T WORRY ABOUT WHAT OTHERS THINK ABOUT YOU.** Don't worry about it because they don't have a heaven or a hell to put you in. They're going to talk about you regardless of whether you're doing bad or good. Remember, you're doing something wrong if they're not talking about you.

10. **DON'T TALK ABOUT IT, BE ABOUT IT!** Actions definitely speak louder than words and that saying goes for your personal and professional life. Many times as women we make the mistake of running our mouths and not doing what we promised ourselves we were going to do. If you say it's over, make sure you keep your word to yourself and make sure it's over. Going back on your word only makes you question yourself. It goes for your career too. If you say you are going to go after your dream, then make it happen. Women who do what they say they're going to do are more successful in life. Remember that your word is your bond.

✦ ABOUT TIONNA

In 2009, Tionna got her big break, teaming up with VH1 to bring her years of hard work and past heartache to the role of the relationship adviser for Rozonda "Chilli" Thomas. Her journey to relationship expert began three years ago with a self-published book that she sent to Gawker.com in hopes that they would cover it. Instead they hired her as their relationship columnist. Her column, "Ask Tionna," received more than 20,000 views daily during its run. Reaching Internet celebrity status, Tionna started hosting her own Internet radio show "Talk Dat Ish" on BlogTalkRadio. She is currently engaged and working on the second season of *What Chilli Wants*.

ACKNOWLEDGMENTS

I want to start out by thanking the two people in my life who have never left my side no matter what: my parents, Tommy and Pamela Smalls. My mother and father are extremely important to me because for one, they birthed me to the world, but secondly because they taught me the game of life and love at a tender age of eight. Thank you, Mommy and Daddy T for all the long-night talks, for allowing us to watch rated-R movies at a young age, and for schooling me and my sisters to the game so we didn't become losers. Thanks for putting a roof over our heads. I'm older now and see that it's not easy to maintain or to show love to another human being. For that alone, you guys have my deepest respect.

To my sisters, Honey, Bunny, and Toni, I thank you for the undying support during the time I was writing this book. I have spoken to you guys a lot about women, men, phony people, and relationships over the past year so I want to thank y'all for just listening and hearing my point of view and for giving me your points of view on these topics. We're sisters and no matter what, we must always stick together.

To my future husband, Gaspar, who I lovingly refer to as "Cas" in public; I would like to thank you for being not only a lover to me but also a friend. You are the best thing that has ever happened to me. You're cool, you're kind, and you're magnificent. I appreciate the love and dedication you show me on a daily basis. You inspire me to be a better woman. You have brought something in my life that has been missing for a very long time and that's simplicity. Yes, baby, your love is simple, never complicated, and I appreciate you for that. You are an addition in my life, never a subtraction, and may God bless our upcoming marriage.

To my family who holds me down no matter what: Grandma Showey, Aunt Mary, Aunt Denise, Uncle Gary, Uncle Lorenzo, Uncle Harry, Cousin June, Cousin Barbra Lesane, Audrey, Regina, Essie, Pop, Matt, Floyd, Curtis, Meek, Tommy, Gary, Tiff, Tasha, Nikki, Sally, Angela, Michael, Marquita, Natasha Drew, my nephew King, my nieces Majesty and Taijae, Antornette, Kiki, Man, Antwan, Naye, and the whole Smalls/Smith family. I love y'all and I want to thank you for being my biggest supporters.

To my extended family: Lydia, Monica, Gaspar Sr., and the rest of the Francis family, I thank you for your love and support and thanks for welcoming me to your family with open arms.

To my real friends and coolest homegirls like Zalika, Arianna, Iyabo, Shatonya, Tiffany Jams, Nisha, Gabi (my hairstylist), Dani, Darenya, CeCe, Tonia, Sparkle, Eve, etc., and my homies Aaron, Handsome Hustler, SB, Joe Columbo, Kenneth, etc., who have supported me from the beginning, thanks for being there for me. Good people are hard to find!

To my assistant, Oateney, what could I have done without you? My interns; my manager, Patrick; my editor, Matthew. My kids at Groundwork, Inc., Street Knowledge Media, Doug and Jackie Christie, Boz and Linda from Ashley Stewart, and the VH1 staff and more, thanks for helping my dreams come true.

Last but not least . . . I want to thank the people who made all of this possible. The ones who read my columns and bought this book and the book before this—my supporters. My fans on Facebook and my followers on Twitter. Y'all kept the name going when everyone else counted me out. I love y'all and I will always make entertainment for you guys because you're my peoples. I talk dat *ish* for you.

To two of the biggest people in my hearts who have since gone on to heaven: my cousin Lavon Smith and my uncle Matthew "Ditto" Jackson. I still can't believe you're gone. There isn't a day I don't think about you both and I know you're looking down on me when my shows come on or when I'm just on the radio. You both supported me from the start and I love and miss you guys. Heaven certainly has two angels. See you at the crossroads.

Thank you, God, for the many blessings and for a humble heart. With his guidance, there will be more books, shows, and mentorship work from Tionna Smalls coming your way. God bless you all. And if I forgot anyone, please blame my mind and not my heart! Peace.